Sugarcraft
FLOWERS

Sugarcraft
FLOWERS

THE ART OF CREATING BEAUTIFUL FLORAL EMBELLISHMENTS

Marilyn Hill

Contents

Introduction

Learning how to make exquisite, realistic sugar flowers and foliage is easy with this fully illustrated step-by-step guide. Whether you're a complete beginner or experienced in sugarcraft, the clear, easy-to-follow instructions and photographs will give you all the information you need.

I recommend that you read through the tools, materials and techniques chapters before you start to make any of the flowers or foliage. There you'll find advice and information on all the tools and materials I have used for the projects, plus detailed instructions on how to work with flower paste. I have developed my own version of flower paste, and you'll find the recipe for this on page 18. In the techniques section you'll also find guidance on the different methods for wiring petals and leaves, and the various stages that you will need to work through to create the individual pieces.

The flowers and foliage I make are all botanically correct, so throughout the projects I refer to the parts of each one by their proper names. You'll find a useful diagram of a flower on page 10, with all its components labelled. Because they are botanically correct, you won't always find suitable cutters to purchase. Therefore templates are provided on pages 144–45, and an explanation on how to use them on page 24. If you need larger or smaller templates, they can be reduced or enlarged on a photocopier.

Finally, you will find a chapter on flower arrangements with eight striking designs to make that can be used for decorating special-occasion cakes. I hope you will find them inspirational and that they will encourage you to be creative in your own arrangements. There are so many unique and innovative ways that you can display sugar flowers and foliage, so have fun experimenting.

I hope that you enjoy this book and that, by following my instructions, you will be able to improve your skills and produce some amazing sugar flowers and projects for yourself.

Marilyn Hill

Before you Start

The Anatomy of Flowers

Throughout the instructions in the projects, you will see references to the botanical parts of a flower. The illustrations below have all these parts labelled. It's a good idea to familiarize yourself with the terminology, and if at any time you're unsure, you can refer back to this page to remind you.

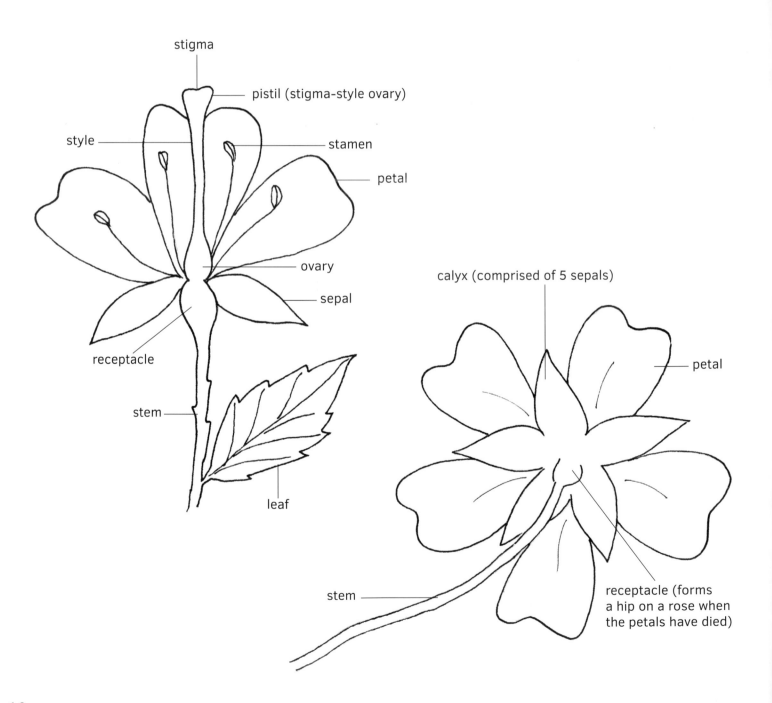

Materials

At the beginning of each project, you will find all the materials you need listed. The names of the dusting colours are specific to the particular brands I have used. This information is provided so that you can match the projects exactly; you can, of course, use alternative colours and brands if you prefer.

Edible glaze

A commercial spray glaze is used to spray flower paste leaves or shiny petals. This gives a natural sheen to the surface of the leaf. The spray should be used in a well-ventilated room or outdoors.

❶ Edible colours *(shown on page 12)*

A wide range of edible colours is used throughout the book. These can be in the form of dusting colours, liquid, paste or gel colours that can be mixed with the flower paste to produce coloured flower paste, or to add colouration to petals and leaves. There are hundreds of shades of dusting powders available from several different manufacturers, so it is easy to produce the colour or shade of flower or foliage required. The dusting powders can also be mixed to provide different shades or tones and diluted with white or darkened with black.

❷ Edible glue *(shown on page 12)*

A commercial product is available; however, I make a similar product by dissolving 1tsp (5ml) of tylose powder (carboxymethyl cellulose) in 3½fl oz (100ml) of water.

❸ Wires *(shown on page 12)*

Available in white or green, wires come in various gauges from 18 to 33. The larger the number, the finer the wire. I prefer to use Japanese Sunrise wires, because the paper covering on these wires does not unravel when in use. I have mainly used white wires, as they can be used for both petals and leaves. I find the green wire too dark to use on leaves, as it shows through.

❹ Polystyrene balls *(shown on page 13)*

These are used as a former in the production of large roses to cut down on the weight and quantity of flower paste used and to simplify the complexity of the centre of the rose. The size I have used is 1½in (4cm) in diameter.

❺ White vegetable fat or petal base
(shown on page 13)

This product is used to soften flower paste to remove cracks and to produce a smooth flower paste. I use it in my version of flower paste (see page 18) and with dusting powders to colour flower paste – a small amount of white fat is added to the powder colour to aid distribution of the powder into the flower paste. Petal base is a commercially available product with a pleasant vanilla smell; it can be used in the same way as white vegetable fat.

❻ Posy picks

These are food-safe plastic flower holders into which floral arrangements can be inserted. The posy pick is inserted into the surface of the coating on the cake.

❼ Gum arabic

This is an edible powder form of the natural gum also known as Acacia gum. When dissolved in water it can be used as an edible glaze, adhesive or thickener.

❽ Acrylic sheet

This is used to make the templates of petals and leaves. This clear plastic material is often used in packaging – for example, on chocolates, boxes of cards or general see-through material used to package household items. I tend to salvage acrylic sheets and store them in a large envelope for future use.

❾ Flower tape

This is available in half width or full width and in a wide range of colours. I have specified the brand and colour used for each flower or foliage project. The tapes can be cut down to quarter width using a tape shredder (see page 17). It is good practice to keep the tape in a polythene bag to prevent the glue in the tape from drying out.

❿ Stamens

Different types, sizes and colours are available commercially. They are non-edible. It is best to use either white or cream, as these can be dusted for each flower to colour them appropriately. The pearlized versions are only suitable for making fantasy flowers.

⑪ Flower paste

There are several pastes available in a wide range of colours from sugarcraft suppliers. However, I make my own version of flower paste, the recipe for which is given on page 18. This produces a white paste that can be coloured with edible colouring materials.

Tools

You will find an array of tools available to purchase from sugarcraft outlets. The specific tools I have used to make the flowers and foliage in this book are detailed below, and a list of suppliers for them is on page 146. It is useful to gather all these items so they're near to hand before you start making.

❶ Cornflour bag

A cornflour (cornstarch) bag is used to dust the surface of the board when petals or leaves are to be cut out. You can buy this, but a homemade version can easily be made from a 4in (10cm) square of muslin into which is placed a tablespoon (15g) of cornflour. The bag is sealed with an elastic band.

❷ Templates

Templates are produced from acrylic sheets as replicas of leaves and petals. These ensure that the flower or leaf is botanically correct. Templates have been used widely throughout the book (see page 24).

❸ Sugarfacts size guide

This plastic guide is punched with circular holes varying in size from 1 to 16. it is used to measure the size of flower paste ball required for each petal or leaf.

❹ Cutters

A wide range of metal and plastic cutters is available for most sizes of petals or leaves. The ones you need are specified at the start of each project. Where a botanically correct cutter is unavailable, templates are specified and provided at the back of the book.

❺ Cel sticks

There are various sizes of Cel sticks available, which are used like small rolling pins. The smaller ones can be used for frilling petal edges; however, you could also use cocktail sticks for this task.

❻ Non-stick rolling pin

Rolling pins of different thicknesses are available. They are used to apply pressure to the flower paste to enable it to be rolled out thinly. A thicker rolling pin allows you to apply more pressure to the flower paste and is often used for larger petals and leaves.

❼ Fine scissors

Used to snip into flower paste to give texture to buds or to produce fine hairs on the sepals of the calyx of roses. They should be sharp and have very fine points.

❽ Scalpel or craft knife

This sharp tool can be used instead of the wheel tool for cutting out petals or leaves and for producing fine cuts on petals or sepals. It has the disadvantage that it will permanently mark the non-stick board.

❾ Wheel tool

Used to cut out shapes (templates), this plastic tool will not damage the surface of a non-stick board (unlike a craft knife). It can also be used to define fine lines on buds or any solid surface.

Digital scales

Scales are required to weigh the quantities of the ingredients used to make the flower paste. Digital scales are the most accurate.

Electric mixer

You will need a heavy-duty electric mixer to make the flower paste. This should be fitted with a dough hook to prevent damage to the motor.

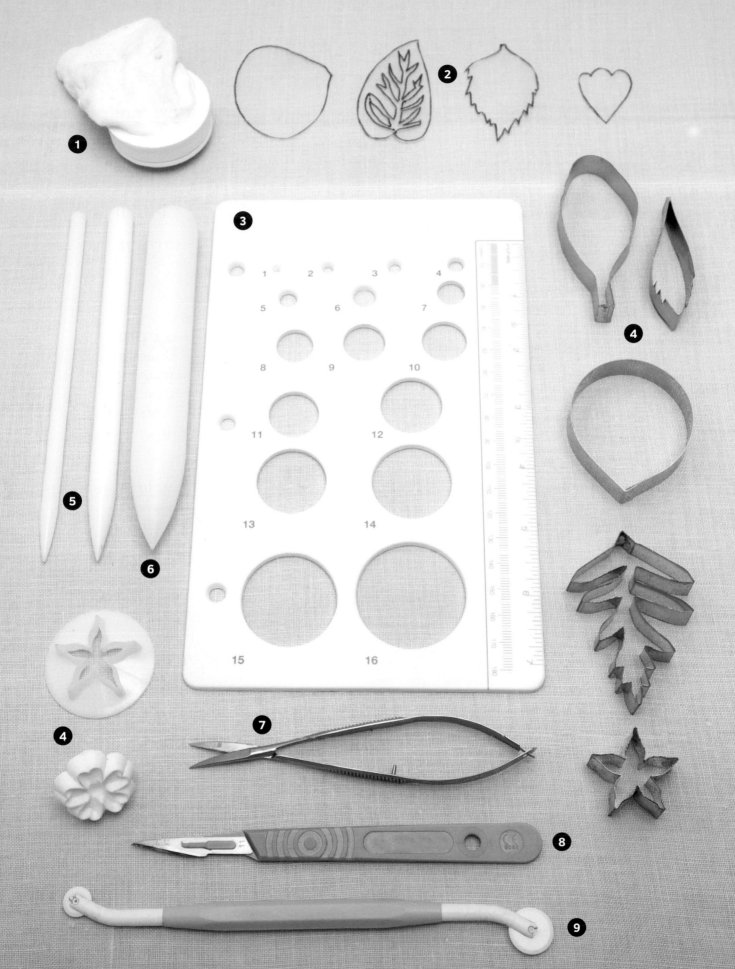

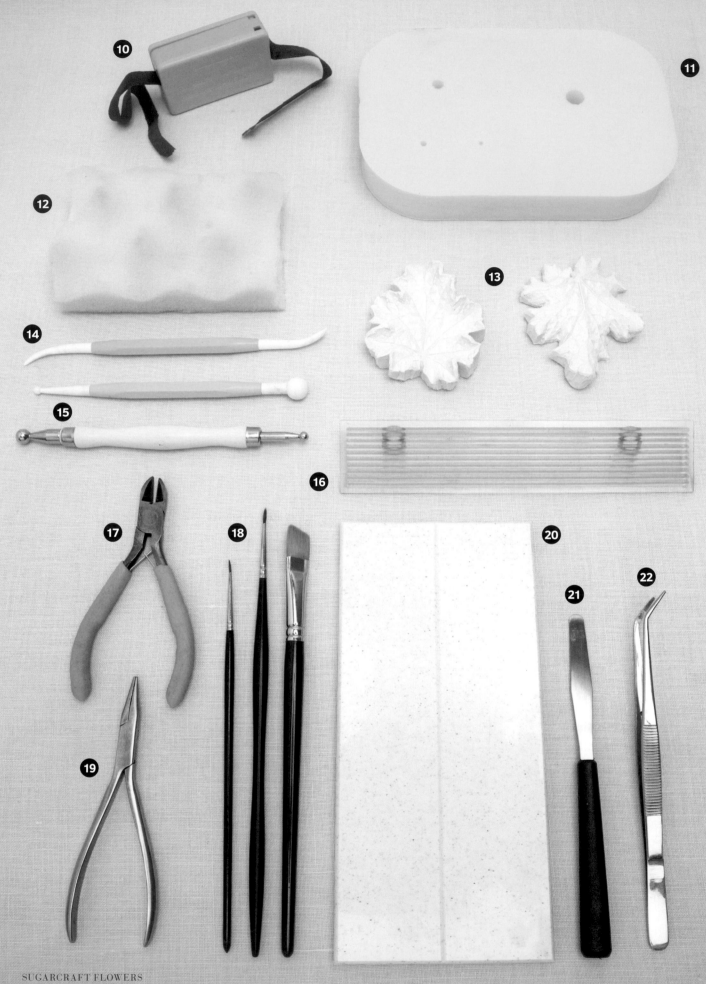

⑩ Tape shredder

This is used to cut flower tape into different widths by adjusting the razor blades inside. The tape is pulled through from one side to the other and emerges as half-width, third-width or quarter-width.

⑪ Foam pad

This block of hard foam is used as a support for the flower or petal when working with the ball tool to thin and flute petal or leaf edges. One with holes is most useful; this can be used, for example, when producing a hip on the back of a rose calyx. I prefer to use a yellow pad produced by CelCakes or a blue version produced by PME.

⑫ Bumpy foam

Bumpy foam is used as a support for bent petals and leaves to maintain their shape during drying.

⑬ Veiners

These are double-sided silicone moulds. The flower paste petal or leaf is positioned centrally inside the mould. Pressure is applied to the top of the mould, which then impresses the paste with the pattern. Veiners greatly improve the look of your work and are essential for producing botanically correct sugar flowers and foliage. It is best to purchase the largest version available, as it can be used for both large and small petals and leaves.

⑭ Dresden tool

This is used to mark central veins in a leaf or petal or to draw out leaf edges to produce a serrated effect.

⑮ Ball tool

The ball tool is used to soften petal and leaf edges and is used in conjunction with a foam pad. The ball tool can be made of metal or plastic. I prefer to use a metal one because it is heavier, so more pressure can be applied to the paste, and is always cool, even in hot weather, so the ball does not stick to the paste.

⑯ Ribbon strip cutter

These plastic devices are available in three widths. For the Old-Fashioned Double Rose on page 76, I used the middle-sized one to cut out strips of flower paste to form the intricate rose centre. They can also be used to produce edible ribbons for cake decorating.

⑰ Wire cutters

Small-sized wire cutters are available from most hardware stores and are used to cut wires to appropriate lengths.

⑱ Brushes

Flat ½in (1.25cm) chisel-shaped synthetic brushes are used to apply dusting colours to petals and leaves. The flat edge of the brush allows the powder to be applied strongly to the edge of the petal or leaf, then blended away across the surface of the paste. It is best to have a range of brushes for different colours.

Sable brushes are used for painting details onto petals or leaves. The more expensive brushes are recommended because they produce a fine point when wet. Sizes vary from 000 to 2, and will be specified in the projects.

A small, inexpensive camel-hair brush can be used to apply edible glue (see page 12).

⑲ Fine-nosed pliers

Stronger than angled tweezers, they can be used in a similar way when assembling large flowers or foliage.

⑳ Large non-stick grooved Cel board

A single long groove on this board produces a ridge on the back of petals and leaves. A wire can then be inserted into the ridge to fully wire the petal or leaf, acting as a support and allowing it to be bent.

㉑ Small palette knife

A small, thin palette knife is used to remove flower paste, petals or leaves from the non-stick board without distorting the petal or leaf.

㉒ Angled tweezers

These help with the assembly of flower or foliage sprays, particularly for adjusting individual pieces within a spray, thus reducing the risk of breakage.

Electric steamer

This is used to steam finished flowers and leaves. It sets the dusting powder onto the surface of the flower paste. The one I use is produced by PME.

Techniques

From making and colouring flower paste to using cutters, templates and other tools, all the techniques you'll need to master are detailed on the following pages. If you are new to making sugar flowers, make sure you read through this section carefully before embarking on any of the projects.

Flower paste

The medium used to make the flowers and foliage in this book is flower paste. Commercial pastes are available from most cake decorating shops. However, I prefer to make my own. I have perfected the recipe over many years, and you will find the ingredients and instructions below.

Flower paste recipe

Ingredients

2fl oz (60ml) boiling water

1oz (25g) powdered gelatine (I use two packets of Dr. Oetker's gelatine powder)

2oz (50g) liquid glucose

2oz (50g) white vegetable fat, plus extra to grease your hands

2lb (900g) icing sugar

1oz (25g) gum tragacanth

Whites of two large eggs

Method

1 Place the water and gelatine in a container (a cup or beaker). Stir well and place the container in a saucepan of boiling water. Allow the gelatine to dissolve.

2 Add the liquid glucose and vegetable fat to this mixture. Heat until the fat has dissolved.

3 Place the icing sugar in a bowl and heat in a microwave on full power for two minutes to warm through.

4 Attach the dough hook to a heavy-duty mixer. Add the icing sugar and gum tragacanth. Stir well.

5 Turn the mixer to a low speed and add the hot gelatine mix, immediately followed by the egg whites. When all of the icing sugar has been incorporated, turn the mixer to speed 3 and beat for three minutes. The mix should be soft and stringy.

6 Divide the mixture into two (it is easier to work with half of the mixture at a time). Place it on a sheet of cling-film. Grease your hands with a little vegetable fat and knead the paste into a smooth ball. Recombine the two halves into one ball.

7 Wrap the paste in cling film and then place in a polythene bag.

8 Place the paste in a fridge and leave for 24 hours before use. The paste can be stored in a fridge for up to a month. It can also be frozen.

Working with flower paste

Flower paste should be stored in a refrigerator or freezer, as it does not contain a preservative. When working with it, it should be at room temperature. A very small amount of white vegetable fat can be added to the paste to soften it, allowing it to be kneaded by hand and removing any cracks. If you accidentally make it too soft, add a small amount of cornflour to firm it up.

When not in use, the paste should be covered in cling-film and placed in a polythene bag to prevent it from drying out and forming a crust on the surface of the paste.

Tip

For best results, it is important to keep all equipment very clean. Make sure you clean your work surfaces with antibacterial wipes and wash your hands before working with flower paste. Also, avoid wearing fluffy jumpers, as hairs from the jumper can get into the paste!

Colouring the flower paste

There is a wide range of edible colouring materials available in the form of pastes, gels, liquid droplets and powders. All of these can be used to colour flower paste. For petals, I use dusting colours to which I add a small quantity of white vegetable fat to aid distribution of the dust through the paste.

For leaves, I use fern drop liquid colour (by Sugarflair) as a base colour, as this produces a very natural-looking green. Flower paste can also be bought ready coloured, as has been used in a few of the projects.

Wiring flowers and foliage

All of the flowers and foliage in this book are fully wired. I have used the large version of the grooved board produced by CelCrafts to produce a ridge on the back of petals or leaves into which a wire is housed. However, there are other methods available to wire petals and leaves, which are detailed below.

Ridge method using a grooved Cel board

1 Roll out a ball of well-kneaded flower paste thinly with a non-stick rolling pin over the groove of a lightly greased non-stick board. If you are using a cutter, remove the paste from the board with a fine palette knife, dust the board with cornflour, turn the paste over and replace it on the dry surface. Cut out the petal or leaf with the cutter, ensuring that the ridge runs down the centre of the petal.

2 If you are using a template, leave the paste in place and position the template on the surface of the paste so that the groove runs down the centre of the template. Then use a wheel tool or a craft knife to cut out the shape.

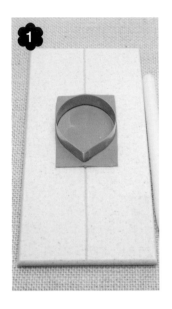

Ridge method without a grooved board

1 Place a ball of flower paste on a lightly greased non-stick board. Use a small rolling pin to press down the paste from the centre to the edge of the paste on one side. Repeat this with the other side. This leaves a ridge in the centre of the paste that will house the wire.

2 Insert the wire into the ridge, then use a cutter or a template to cut out the petal or leaf.

Sandwich method

1 Roll out a ball of well-kneaded flower paste on a lightly greased non-stick board. Position half a length of wire halfway up the paste, long enough for the length of the petal or leaf.

2 Bring down the remaining piece of paste to encase the wire in the paste. Then roll the paste together on either side of the wire with a small rolling pin. You can then use a cutter or a template to cut out the petal or leaf.

Tip

Cut wires at an angle to make inserting the wire into the flower paste easier. Do not bend wires in two and then cut them, as this leaves a bend in the wire that will need to be cut off.

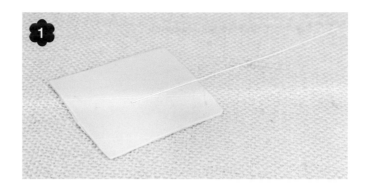

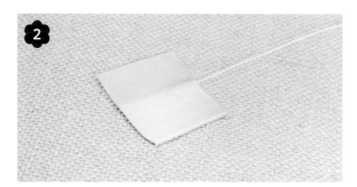

Solid paste method

1 Use this method for large petals or leaves more than 3in (7.5cm) long. Roll a ball of paste into a long sausage shape. Insert a wire into the centre of the sausage shape from the base to the top.

2 Place the sausage shape on a lightly greased non-stick board. Carefully roll out the paste lengthways and then sideways on either side of the wire. Then use a cutter or a template to cut out the petal or leaf.

Tip

Greasing the board with a little white fat holds the paste in place so that you can apply more pressure with the rolling pin.

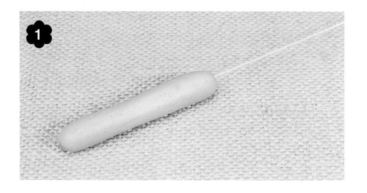

Stick and twist method

1 Push half a length of wire into a small ball of well-kneaded flower paste. Position the ball of paste 2in (5cm) along the length of the wire.

2 Roll the paste up the wire, either with your fingers or by rolling the paste on a non-stick board, until the wire is covered with a thin layer of paste. Remove excess paste from the top of the wire with your nails.

3 Cut out the petal or leaf with a cutter or template and place it flat on a non-stick board. Dampen the paste-covered wire with water and stick it to the centre back of the petal or leaf, ensuring that the length of the petal or leaf is covered. Remove any excess paste from the base.

4 Place the wired petal or leaf between a pair of double-sided veiners. Apply pressure to the top veiner so that the wire sticks firmly to the back of the petal or leaf and that good veining is achieved.

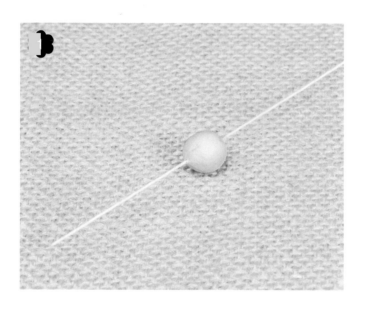

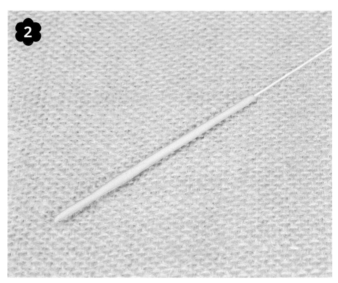

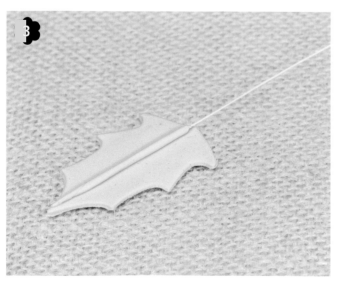

Using cutters

Cutters for most common flowers are available in either metal or plastic. It is essential that the cutters are clean before use, or your petals or leaves will have burred edges.

Cut out the petals and leaves on a dry surface. Lightly dust the board with cornflour to enable you to cut out the items cleanly.

Tip

It is useful to label all your cutters with a permanent marker pen, as it can be difficult to remember what each cutter is for.

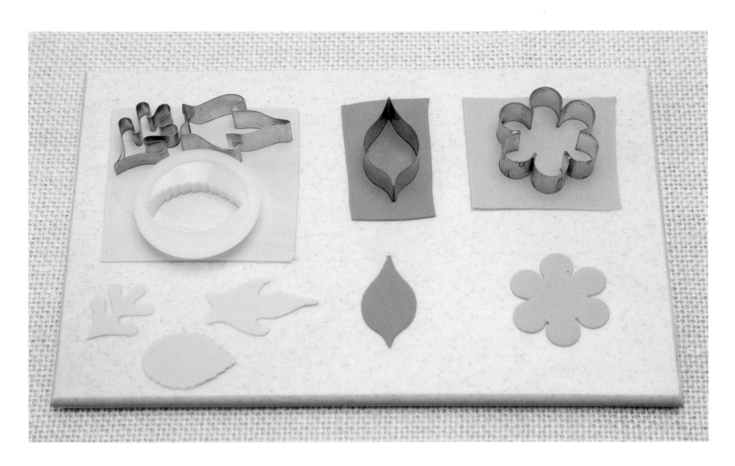

Ribbon strip cutter

This plastic device is used to produce precise strips of flower paste. Roll out a ball of well-kneaded flower paste on a lightly greased non-stick board, using a non-stick rolling pin. Remove the paste and place on a surface that has been dusted with cornflour. Place the strip cutter on top of the flower paste and push down firmly so that it cuts into the paste and fills the section in the cutter. Turn the strip cutter over so that the strips of paste can be removed.

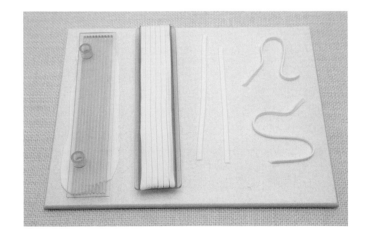

Templates

If the correct size or shape of cutter is not available, you will need to make a template using an actual petal or leaf from the flower or plant you want to recreate. Using a template produces botanically correct petals and leaves and can be more cost effective than purchasing cutters.

1 Use clear acrylic sheet and a fine permanent marker pen. Place a piece of acrylic sheet over the petal or leaf and draw around the shape with the marker pen.

2 Cut out the shape with a pair of fine scissors and label the template.

Larger or smaller templates can be produced by drawing uniformly outside or inside the original shape, or by using a photocopier to increase or decrease the size of the image.

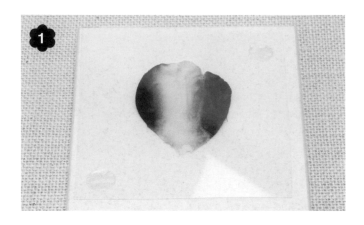

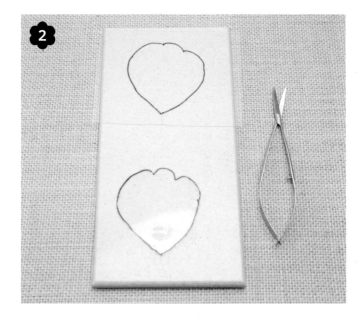

Veining

Petals and leaves can be veined after they have been wired using double-sided petal and leaf veiners. Place the petal or leaf centrally in between the two halves of the veiner and apply pressure with your fingers to the top veiner, pressing down hard to achieve good veining.

Tip
Wipe veiners with a paper towel after use to keep them clean.

Using a ball tool

The ball tool is used to soften petal and leaf edges and to give the edges movement. Place the petal or leaf on a hard foam pad and rub the ball tool against the edges, working half on the petal or leaf edge and half on the foam pad.

Where the petal needs to be frilled or fluted to give slight movement to the petal edge, place the petal on a non-stick board that has been dusted with cornflour, then apply pressure to the petal or leaf edge with the ball tool, working half on the edge and half on the board. Working on a hard surface gives more movement to the edge than just softening the edge on a foam pad.

Frilling

This technique is used for any petal with a frilled edge. Place the petal on a non-stick board lightly dusted with cornflour. Apply pressure to the petal edge with a small Cel or cocktail stick, rolling it backwards and forwards along the edge of the petal that requires frilling.

Colouring petals and leaves

It is best to colour petals and leaves before they dry, as the dusting colours adhere better to damp paste. Powders can be mixed to obtain the precise colour you want, as colours straight from the pot are not always the exact shade required.

The dusting powders can be placed in a plastic painting palette or on a piece of greaseproof paper, which will not absorb the colour. Any excess colour can be brushed back into the pot.

Using wide, chisel-shaped synthetic brushes is best, as they hold the powder better than sable brushes and are far cheaper. When dusting, work from the petal or leaf edge inwards. This gives the edge a stronger colour and avoids any solid lines on the petal or leaf. When dusting buds, work from the top to the base. This prevents any harsh lines of colour on your work.

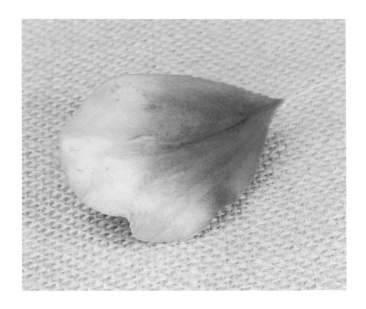

Tip

To clean a brush, dip it in cornflour (cornstarch) and rub the dusting colour off onto a piece of towelling. If you need to wash the brush, wash it with standard shampoo followed by conditioner. Never leave a brush standing in water, as this will bend the hairs and they will not recover. Allow the brush to dry thoroughly before you put it away.

Spots, dashes or fine-painted lines

You can apply these to the petal or leaf with a fine (size 00) sable brush, using any of the commercially available edible colours. The dusting powders can be dissolved in any drinkable clear alcohol or water.

Tip

It is always useful to have some spare petals or leaves that you can use to practise your painting skills on, or to try out your brush, rather than spoiling a valuable petal or leaf.

Steaming

Once the flower or leaf has been coloured and the flower assembled, it needs to be steamed to set the dusting powder colours onto the surface of the paste. This is particularly important if you are using the flowers to decorate a cake, as the dust could fall on the cake covering. Steaming is achieved by quickly passing the completed flower or leaf through a jet of steam. Commercial steamers are available from PME.

Tip

Always hold the item by the end of the stem. Have the jet of steam emerging from the device away from you and pass the item quickly through the steam. It is safer to steam the finished piece taped together rather than small individual items. You can wear protective gloves if you wish.

Glazing

Some leaves, such as holly and laurel, are shiny. An edible spray can be used to achieve this effect on the surface of a sugar leaf. There are several companies that produce glaze in aerosol form, the most popular being from PME. This process should be carried out in a well-ventilated room or in the open air once the leaf has been steamed.

Taping

The flower tape most commonly used in this book is half-width Nile green, produced by Hamilworth. Flower tape comes in a variety of colours and in full or half-widths (known as split tape because it comes as two lots of half-widths in a pack). Tape shredders are also available that will cut full-width tape into different widths.

Quarter-width tape is used when taping small, delicate flowers together. It is produced by cutting half-width tape into two lengthwise with a tape shredder or scissors.

It is important to stretch the tape as you tape down the wires to form a stem. Do this by holding the stem in one hand and the tape in the other and twisting the wire stem either clockwise or anticlockwise, at the same time pulling on the tape with the fingers of your other hand. This produces a smooth stem and does not have a bandaged effect.

Some flowers and leaves do not have green stems. In this case, white flower tape is used, then dusted with the appropriate colour using dusting powders.

Tip

If the tape breaks when you're using it, this means it is old and the glue in it has dried out. It should be discarded.

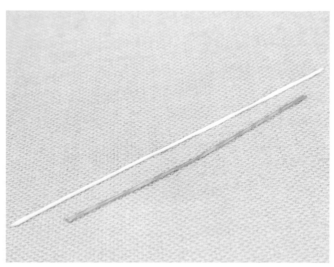

Flowers

Camellia

One of the most popular winter- and spring-flowering shrubs, camellias provide colour in the garden when there is little else in bloom. The flowers are usually white, pink or red in colour. There are single, double, peony and rose forms. The one shown here is a rose form.

Materials and Equipment

Pink flower paste coloured with pink dusting powder (EdAble Art)

Pale green flower paste coloured with fern droplet liquid colour (Sugarflair)

KM 24 cream stamens (The Old Bakery)

28# and 24# white Sunrise wires (The Old Bakery)

Half-width Nile green and beige flower tapes (Hamilworth)

Sunflower and peony rose dusting powders (EdAble Art)

Vine green and nutkin brown dusting powders (Squires Kitchen)

Hunter green dusting powder (Diamond)

Rose petal cutters, ¾in (2cm), 1in (2.5cm) and 1¼in (3cm) wide from set 582 (Fine Cut Sugarcraft Products)

Large rose leaf cutters 576 and 577 (Fine Cut Sugarcraft Products)

Camellia petal veiner (Squires Kitchen)

Hibiscus leaf veiner (Ellen's Creative Sugarcraft)

Edible glue (homemade from tylose powder; see page 11)

Edible spray glaze (PME)

Sugarcraft tools (see pages 14–17)

Tip
The size of your camellia will depend on which size of rose petal cutter you choose – here, I used 1in (2.5cm) and 1¼in (3cm) wide cutters.

Method

Stamen assembly (centre)

1 Take 15 stamens and double them over to give 30 heads. Place half a length of 28# wire alongside, with ½in (1.25cm) protruding above the stamen heads. Using quarter-width Nile green flower tape (half-width tape cut into two with a tape shredder or scissors), bind around the stamens and wire.

2 Pull the end of the wire down over the tape and tape together for a neat effect. Make five groups of stamens in total.

3 Dust the stamens with sunflower dusting powder on the heads and vine green dusting powder on the cotton section. Use a paintbrush to tip the ends with nutkin brown dusting powder that has been dissolved in a small amount of clear alcohol or water.

4 Fan the stamens out, and tape the groups together to form a complete circle of stamens.

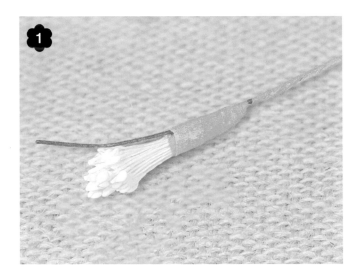

Petals

This camellia has two rows of petals, made from a total of 11 petals using both sizes of rose petal cutters.

5 Roll out a ball of pink flower paste over the groove on a Cel board. Cut out five petals using the 1in (2.5cm) wide rose petal cutter from set 582, placing the ridge in the centre of each petal.

6 Insert half a length of 28# white wire into the base of each petal and push it all the way up to the top of the ridge on the back of the petals. Cut out a small V-shape at the top of each petal using the bottom of the rose petal cutter.

7 Vein each wired petal with a camellia petal veiner. Press down firmly on the top veiner to achieve good veining of the petal. Place the petal on a foam pad and soften the edges of the petal with a ball tool, working half on the petal edge and half on the foam pad.

8 Bend the petal upwards at the base to create space so that the petal will sit under the stamens. Allow to dry for ten minutes, resting the petals on bumpy foam to keep their shape.

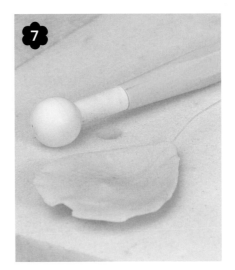

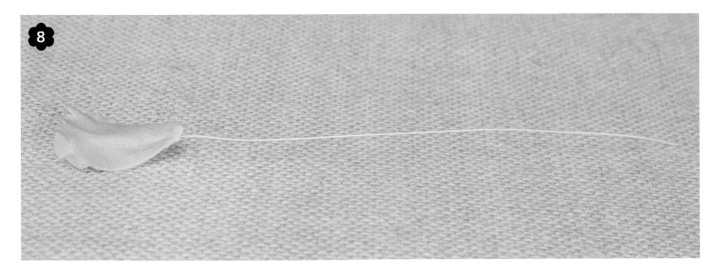

9 Dust the top surface of the petals all over with peony rose dusting powder, using a chisel-shaped brush and working from the outside edge inwards.

10 Attach a length of half-width Nile green flower tape to the base of the stamens. Tape each petal in underneath the stamens. Rearrange them if necessary, so that they fit neatly without any gaps.

11 Repeat steps 1–5 using the 1¼in (3cm) wide rose petal cutter from set 582. Make six petals. Using half-width Nile green flower tape, tape these petals onto the stem immediately underneath the first row of petals, placing them in between the petals of the first row.

Calyx

12 Roll out a ball of pale green flower paste on a lightly greased non-stick board. Cut out six small rose petal shapes using a ¾in (2cm) rose petal cutter from set 582. These will be the sepals. Place them on a foam pad and thin the edges using a ball tool. Ball the centre of each with the ball tool.

13 Glue each sepal in place in the centre of each petal, spacing them evenly around the base of the back of the flower. Allow to partially dry, then dust the centre of each sepal with hunter green dusting powder, leaving the edges pale.

Bud

14 Take a size 9 (Sugarfacts guide) piece of pink flower paste. Roll the paste into a ball and insert half a length of 24# white wire into the top of the ball. Pull the wire down through the paste.

15 Reshape the top of the ball to hide the wire, then insert three more half-lengths of 24# white wires into the centre of the ball from the base end. Use a wheel tool to mark the top of the bud into three sections.

16 Tape the wires together with half-width Nile green flower tape to form the stem. Dust the top of the bud with peony rose dusting powder, using a chisel-shaped brush.

17 Repeat steps 12–13 of the calyx. Apply a thin layer of edible glue to the inside of the sepals and attach the five sepals evenly around the bud.

18 Allow to dry for ten minutes, then dust the centre of each sepal with hunter green petal dust, leaving a pale edge on each sepal.

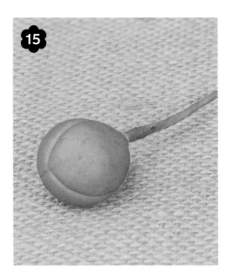

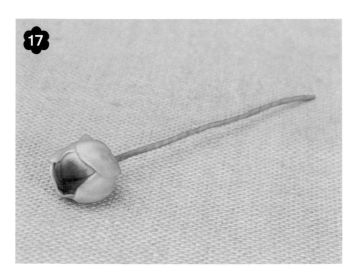

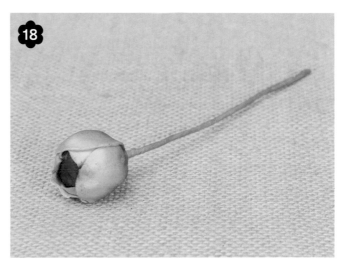

Leaves

19 Roll out a ball of pale green flower paste over the groove of a non-stick Cel board. Cut out several leaves using the two sizes of rose leaf cutters. Insert a quarter-length of 28# white wire into the ridge on the back of each leaf.

20 Vein the leaves using a hibiscus leaf veiner. Thin the edges of each leaf with a ball tool on a foam pad.

21 Bend the wire inside the leaf backwards to give movement, then allow the leaves to dry on bumpy foam to maintain their shape.

22 Dust the top surface of the leaf with a mixture of hunter green and nutkin brown dusting powders. Pass the dusted leaf quickly through a jet of steam from an electric steamer to set the dusting powder onto the surface of the paste.

23 Spray each leaf with edible spray glaze to give the leaves a shine. Do this outside or in a well-ventilated room. Attach a quarter-length of 24# white wire to the base of each leaf and tape together with half-width beige flower tape, taping down the wires to form a stem.

24 Attach a leaf to the camellia bud with half-width beige flower tape. Attach this to the stem behind the flower. Add two more leaves at the same point on the stem. Tape down the stem with half-width beige flower tape to complete the flower spray. Pass the spray quickly through a jet of steam from an electric steamer to set the dusting powders onto the surface of the flower paste.

Red Poppy

Wild poppies, with their bright red, tissue-paper-thin petals, are a striking sight when seen en masse. They are annuals that flower in the summer, generally in arable fields or in disturbed ground. They have four petals with a creased, silky appearance, and two sepals, which fall off as the flower opens. Poppies are traditionally used as a symbol of remembrance, as during the First World War they were one of the few flowers to bloom on the battlefields.

Materials and Equipment

Pale green flower paste coloured with fern droplet liquid colour (Sugarflair)

Red flower paste (A Piece of Cake)

Small KM 15 black stamens (The Old Bakery)

30#, 28#, 26# and 24# white Sunrise wires (The Old Bakery)

Half-width Nile green flower tape (Hamilworth)

Liquorice black paste colour (Sugarflair)

Poppy red dusting powder (Squires Kitchen)

Hunter green dusting powder (Diamond)

Red poppy petal template (see page 145)

Poppy leaf cutter (Tinkertech Two)

Poppy petal and leaf veiners (Squires Kitchen)

Sugarcraft tools (see pages 14–17)

Method

Seed box centre (ovary)

1 Take a size 6 (Sugarfacts guide) piece of pale green flower paste. Roll it into a ball and then into a cone shape. Insert half a length of 26# white wire into the pointed end of the cone and pinch the paste onto the wire to secure the seed box.

2 Flatten the top and pinch in eight ridges (like the spokes of a wheel) on the top of the seed box, using a pair of fine tweezers. Paint the ridges with liquorice black paste colour diluted with water or alcohol using a fine sable brush.

3 Take 20 black stamens, double them over and attach to a one-third length of 30# white wire. Make three groups of stamens for each flower.

4 Attach these stamen assemblies to the base of the seed box, using quarter-width Nile green flower tape (half-width tape cut into two with a tape shredder or scissors). Use a pair of fine tweezers to arrange the stamens evenly around the seed box centre.

Petals

5 Roll out a ball of red flower paste over the groove on a Cel board. Place the petal template over the paste on the board so that the groove runs down the centre of each petal. Cut out four petals for each flower, using

a wheel tool or scalpel. Take one of the petals and insert half a length of 30# white wire into the ridge on the back of the petal. Vein the petal with the poppy petal veiner. Repeat for the other three petals.

6 Place the wired petal on a foam pad and thin the edges of the petal, working with a ball tool placed half on the petal edge and half on the foam pad. Curve the petal backwards by bending the wire within the petal. Make four petals for each flower.

7 Allow all the petals to partially dry for ten minutes, then dust them with poppy red dusting powder using a chisel-shaped brush. Work from the outside edge inwards until the whole of the petal is dusted.

Assembly

8 Attach a length of half-width Nile green flower tape to the base of the poppy centre. Tape in two petals opposite each other and under the seed box centre, using the green flower tape. Stretch the tape and twist the flower so that the stem is covered with a thin layer of tape.

9 Tape in the other two petals at right angles to the first petals. Adjust the petals so that they fit well together. Add three extra half-lengths of 24# white wires to the stem to make the stem thicker and to give the flower support. Tape all the way down the stem, as before, with half-width Nile green flower tape.

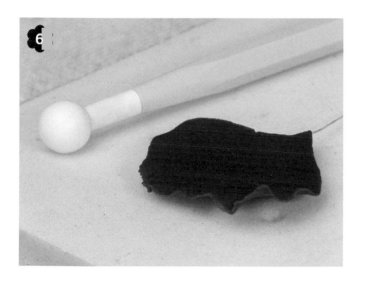

Flower bud

10 Roll a size 8 (Sugarfacts guide) piece of well-kneaded pale green flower paste into an egg shape. Insert half a length of 24# white wire into the wider end of the bud, pinching the paste onto the wire at the base.

11 Using a pair of very fine scissors, make tiny V-shaped cuts all over the surface of the bud to represent the hairy surface.

12 Dust all over the bud with hunter green dusting powder. Add two half-lengths of 24# white wires to the stem, then tape down the stem with half-width Nile green flower tape, stretching the tape so that the stem is covered with a thin layer of tape.

Leaves

13 Roll out a ball of pale green flower paste over the groove on a Cel board. Cut out several leaves using the poppy leaf cutter. Make a few small leaves using just the top part of the cutter. Insert a quarter-length of 28# white wire into the base of the ridge on the back of each leaf. Push and twist the wire to the top of the leaf.

14 Vein the leaf using a poppy leaf veiner. Place on a foam pad and thin the edges of the leaf carefully, as they are quite fragile. Allow to partially dry for ten minutes before dusting the leaves all over with hunter green dusting powder, using a chisel-shaped brush.

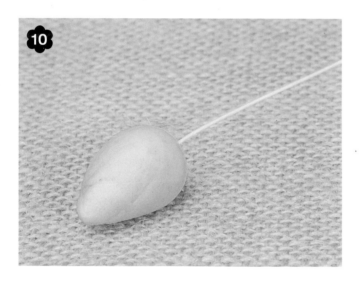

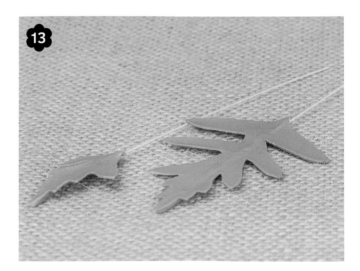

Assembly

15 Attach a length of half-width Nile green flower tape to the bud. Insert a small leaf behind the bud. Tape the bud and leaf together with the green flower tape. Leave the tape attached for the next step.

16 Continue to tape down the stem with half-width Nile green flower tape to make room on the stem for the poppy flower. Attach the poppy flower here. Then tape in a large leaf immediately under the flower. Tape down the stem with the green flower tape. Pass the completed flower spray quickly through a jet of steam to set the coloured dusts onto the surface of the flower paste.

Honeysuckle

This summer-flowering vine can be found in gardens and growing wild in woods and hedgerows. The variety shown here is the cultivated type with pink/cream flowers, but there are at least 20 varieties in Europe and many more in China. The wild variety is cream with apricot and has a wonderful perfume that some of the cultivars sadly lack. Honeysuckle is easy to make using flower paste and could be added to sprays, arrangements or bouquets.

Materials and Equipment

White flower paste

Pale green flower paste coloured with fern droplet liquid colour (Sugarflair)

Fine white micro KM 05 stamens (The Old Bakery)

28# and 24# white Sunrise wires (The Old Bakery)

Half-width white and Nile green flower tapes (Hamilworth)

Peony rose, ginko and honeysuckle dusting powders (EdAble Art)

Hunter green dusting powder (Diamond)

Honeysuckle leaf template (see page 145)

Gardenia leaf veiner

Edible glue (homemade from tylose powder; see page 12)

Sugarcraft tools (see pages 14–17)

Method

Buds

1 Take a size 4 (Sugarfacts guide) piece of well-kneaded white flower paste and roll it into a tapering cone. Insert a one-third length of 28# white wire into the pointed end of the cone and roll the paste onto the wire on your non-stick board. Adjust to a length of 1½in (4cm) by removing any excess paste with your fingers. Tip the free end of the bud over your finger to give it shape.

2 Dust the bud with peony rose dusting powder, working from the top of the bud to the base with a chisel-shaped brush. Make eight buds for each honeysuckle spray.

Calyx

3 Take a tiny piece of pale green flower paste and roll it into a cone shape. Insert a small Cel stick or cocktail stick into the fat end and open it up to make a cup.

4 Insert the wire of the bud through the centre of the cup and stick it in place with a small amount of edible glue. Dust the calyx with ginko dusting powder.

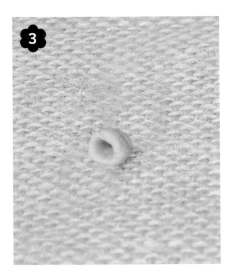

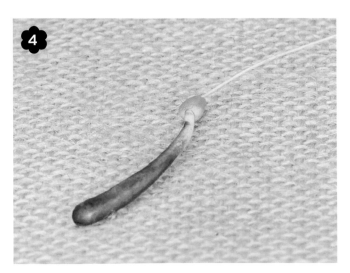

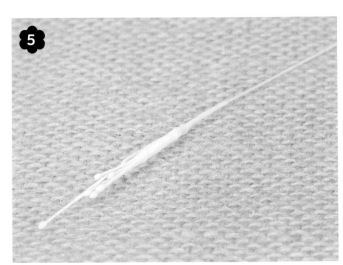

Stamen assembly

5 Take three fine white micro stamens, double them over and attach them to a one-third length of 28# white wire with quarter-width white flower tape (half-width tape cut into two with a tape shredder or scissors).

6 Roll a size 5 (Sugarfacts guide) piece of white flower paste into a tapered cone shape about 1½in (4cm) long. Insert a small Cel stick or cocktail stick into one end until it is about a quarter of the way down the cone. Hold this end against your index finger and use the stick to open up and thin the paste.

7 Using a pair of fine scissors, make two cuts into the paste to make the first petal. Cut away a wedge of paste on either side of the petal.

8 Divide the rest of the paste by making three even-sized cuts. This will make the remaining four petals.

9 Pinch each of the four petals sideways with your finger and thin them with a small Cel stick. Bend the petals backwards.

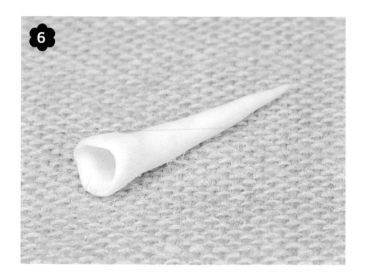

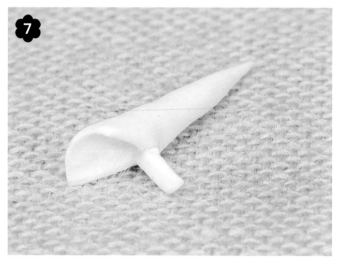

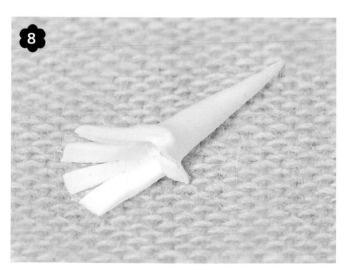

10 Insert the stamen assembly into the hollow tube and pull down so that the stamens just protrude out of the petals. Rub the base of the cone onto the wire to ensure that it is firmly attached. Carefully dust the outside of the floret with peony rose dusting powder, using a chisel-shaped brush. Dust the inside with honeysuckle dusting powder, using a small chisel-shaped brush. Repeat steps 5–10 to make five more florets.

11 Make and attach a calyx for each floret as for the bud.

Flower assembly

12 Attach a length of half-width Nile green flower tape to the base of a bud. Place the remaining six buds next to this and tape in at the same level. Arrange these into a neat cluster. Tape in six florets behind the buds, with the long, narrow petal facing down. Tape down the stem with the tape.

Leaves

13 Roll out a piece of pale green flower paste over the groove of a lightly greased Cel board. Place the leaf template (see page 145) over the groove and cut out four leaves. Remove the leaves from the board and insert a quarter-length piece of 28# white wire into the ridge at the back of each leaf.

14 Vein the leaf with a gardenia leaf veiner, then soften the edges with a ball tool working on a foam pad. Dust the front surface of the leaf with a mix of ginko and hunter green dusting powders.

Leaf assembly

15 Attach a length of half-width Nile green flower tape to half a length of 24# white wire. Tape down the wire for 1in (2.5cm), stretching the tape as you work down the wire to form a stem. Tape in one leaf on either side of the stem, and tape down the stem for 2in (5cm).

16 Attach the bud assembly at this point, taping the bud in firmly with half-width Nile green flower tape.

17 Continue to tape down the stem for another 2in (5cm), then tape in the flower followed by a pair of leaves. Tape down the stem to complete the honeysuckle spray.

Foxglove

These wild flowers are found in white and magenta with dark magenta spots. The plants can grow to 6ft (1.8m) tall and consist of a series of small buds at the top of a spike opening to flowers of increasing size down the stem. The leaves grow at the base of the flower in a rosette form. Foxgloves can be found in woodlands, gardens, fields, moorlands, coastal cliffs, roadside verges and waste ground. They are a wonderful source of nectar for bees and moths.

Materials and Equipment

Pale green flower paste coloured with fern droplet liquid colour (Sugarflair)

White flower paste

Small white lily stamens KM 40 (The Old Bakery)

28#, 26# and 24# white Sunrise wires (Old Bakery)

Half-width Nile green flower tape (Hamilworth)

Hunter green dusting powder (Diamond)

Blackcurrant, violet and baby maize dusting powders (EdAble Art)

Burgundy droplet liquid colour (Sugarflair)

Foxglove cutter set 277 (Fine Cut Sugarcraft Products)

Stephanotis petal cutter 628 (Fine Cut Sugarcraft Products)

Foxglove leaf template (see page 144)

Foxglove leaf veiner (Squires Kitchen)

Edible glue (homemade from tylose powder; see page 12)

Sugarcraft tools (see pages 14–17)

Method

Buds

1 Make three small cone-shaped buds of varying sizes with small pieces of pale green flower paste. Make several buds of varying sizes. Insert a quarter-length of 28# white wire into the narrow end of a cone. Pinch the paste at the base onto the wire to secure it. Draw a line around the top of the bud with a wheel tool.

2 Dust the buds with hunter green dusting powder, then dust the tips of the buds with a mixture of blackcurrant and violet dusting powders (magenta mix). Use a chisel-shaped brush and work from the top of the bud to the base.

3 Make two larger buds in the same way, using a size 7 (Sugarfacts guide) piece of white flower paste. Flatten each bud between your fingers, then draw a line with a wheel tool around the fat part of the bud.

4 Take a size 8 (Sugarfacts guide) piece of white flower paste and roll it into a fat cone shape. Insert a thin Cel stick or cocktail stick into the fat end and open this up by rolling the paste across your finger to thin the edge, then push the sides inwards.

5 Insert a short length of 28# white wire to which has been added a small ball of pale green flower paste a few millimetres in from the end. Pull on the wire so that the bud is securely attached.

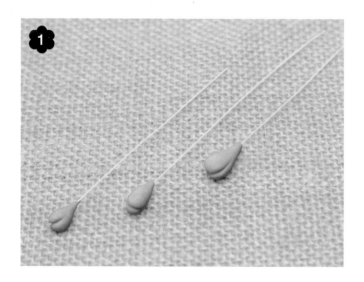

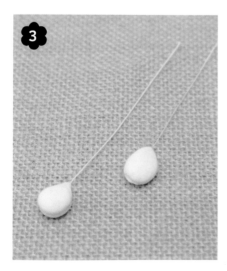

Open flower stamen assembly

6 Take three white lily stamen heads. Dust the stamen heads with baby maize dusting powder, using a chisel-shaped brush. Attach the stamens to a quarter-length of 28# white wire with quarter-width Nile green flower tape (half-width tape cut into two with a tape shredder or scissors). Stretch the tape as you work; this makes the assembly neater. Attach a small piece of pale green flower paste to the base of the stamens and allow to dry.

7 Roll out a size 8 (Sugarfacts guide) piece of white flower paste thinly on a lightly greased non-stick board and cut out a petal using the foxglove cutter. Frill the wide end of the petal with a thin Cel stick or cocktail stick and pull the frilled edge downwards. Place the petal on a foam pad and thin the edges by applying pressure with a ball tool.

8 Apply a thin layer of edible glue to one long edge and carefully fold the paste over to form a tube, overlapping the edges as neatly as possible. It may help to insert a medium-sized Cel stick into the petal to act as a support.

9 Insert the stamen assembly through the top of the flower and pull up into place. Pinch the flower gently at the top to secure it to the wire. Reshape the flower before allowing it to partially dry.

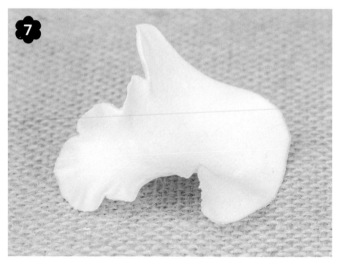

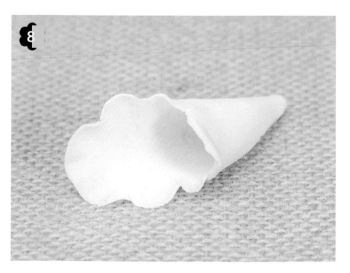

Colouring

10 Dust the large white buds and flowers on the front only with a mixture of blackcurrant and violet dusting powders (magenta mix), using a chisel-shaped brush. Using a size 00 sable brush, paint in small spots with burgundy droplet liquid colour on the lip and back of the open flowers and on the back only of the small white buds.

11 Dust the centre of the back of the flowers and large buds with baby maize dusting powder.

Calyx

12 Roll out some pale green flower paste thinly on a lightly greased non-stick board and cut out a calyx using the stephanotis petal cutter. Thin the edges of the calyx on a foam pad and ball each sepal with a small ball tool. Glue the calyx in place at the base of each flower and bud with edible glue. Dust the calyx with hunter green dusting powder, followed by the magenta mix on the tips.

Leaves

13 Roll out a size 9 (Sugarfacts guide) piece of pale green flower paste thinly over the groove of a lightly greased non-stick Cel board. Place the leaf template (see page 144) over the paste so that the groove runs down the centre of the template. Use a wheel tool to cut around the template.

14 Carefully remove the cut-out leaf from the board. Insert half a length of 26# white wire into the base of the ridge at the back of the leaf. Push and twist the wire up to the top of the leaf.

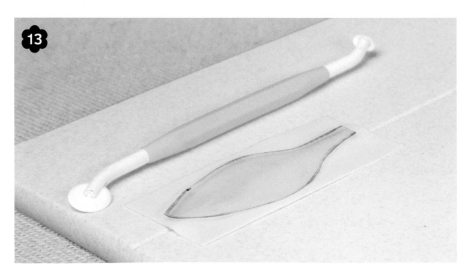

15 Vein the wired leaf with a foxglove leaf veiner, pressing down firmly to achieve good veining.

16 Place the leaf on a foam pad and thin and flute the edges of the leaf by applying pressure to the edge of the leaf with a ball tool, working half on the leaf edge and half on the foam pad.

17 Bend the wire in the leaf backwards slightly to give it movement. Dust the front surface of the leaf only with hunter green dusting powder, using a chisel-shaped brush. Leave the back undusted, as this leaf is paler on the back.

Flower assembly

18 Tape three small buds and three large buds to a 24# white wire using half-width Nile green flower tape, stretching the tape as you tape in the buds and leaving a small gap between each bud. As you go down the stem, this gaps between the buds and each flower will become wider.

19 Add each flower to alternate sides of the stem, at the same time adding in more 24# white wires to strengthen and widen the stem. Add three leaves to the base of the stem, then tape down to cover all wires. Pass the finished flower stem quickly through a jet of steam to set the dusting powders onto the paste.

Wild Rose

During the summer months, wild roses can be seen growing in hedgerows. There are two types: a small cream variety and the more common white with a pale pink edge. The flowers have five even-sized petals. When these petals have fallen off, a hip develops that turns a glorious bright red in the autumn. I have chosen to make the more common variety of wild rose.

Materials and Equipment

Pale green flower paste coloured with fern droplet liquid colour (Sugarflair)

White flower paste

Red flower paste (A Piece of Cake)

Toffee-coloured flower paste coloured with caramel paste colour (Sugarflair)

KM05 micro yellow stamens (The Old Bakery)

30#, 28# and 24# white Sunrise wires (The Old Bakery)

Half-width Nile green flower tape (Hamilworth)

Hunter green dusting powder (Diamond)

Ginko, sunflower, raisin pink and baby maize dusting powders (EdAble Art)

Liquorice black paste colour (Sugarflair)

Wild rose petal template (see page 145)

Small and medium calyx cutters from set 165 (Fine Cut Sugarcraft Products)

Rose leaf cutters set 9324 (Fine Cut Sugarcraft Products)

Rose petal veiner (Squires Kitchen)

Rose leaf veiner (Squires Kitchen)

Edible glue (homemade from tylose powder; see page 12)

Edible glaze (PME)

Sugarcraft tools (see pages 14–17)

Method

Centre and stamen units

Make a centre and stamen unit for every flower required.

1 Take a size 5 (Sugarfacts guide) piece of well-kneaded pale green flower paste and roll it into a ball. Insert half a length of 28# white wire into the base of the ball and pinch the paste at the base onto the wire. Allow to dry, then dust the top of the ball with ginko dusting powder and the sides with sunflower dusting powder.

2 Take 20 micro yellow stamens. Double them over and attach to half a length of 30# white wire with quarter-width Nile green flower tape (half-width tape

cut into two with a tape shredder or scissors). Make three groups. Dust the stamen heads with sunflower dusting powder.

3 Attach a length of half-width Nile green flower tape to the base of the centre and tape in the three stamen units evenly around the centre. Tape down the stem with the green tape.

Petals

4 Roll out a size 10 (Sugarfacts guide) piece of white flower paste over the groove on a lightly greased Cel board. Place the wild rose petal template (see page 145) centrally over the groove. Cut round the template with a wheel tool. Make 10 petals – five

for each flower – in this way. Insert half a length of 28# white wire into the base of each petal, pushing and twisting the wire to the top of each petal. Vein each petal using a rose petal veiner.

5 Place the petals on a foam pad and thin the top edge of each one with a ball tool, working half on the petal and half on the pad. Curve the petals backwards by bending the wire in each one.

6 Allow the petals to partially dry before dusting the top edges with raisin pink dusting powder and the bases with baby maize dusting powder.

Flower assembly

7 To make the first flower, attach a length of half-width Nile green flower tape to the base of the stamen assembly. Tape in three petals so that they form a triangular shape, then tape in the two remaining petals in the gaps.

8 Roll a size 8 (Sugarfacts guide) piece of pale green flower paste into a fat cone. Insert the pointed end into the middle-sized hole of a foam pad and roll over the paste with a small Cel stick. Take the flattened cone out of the pad, turn it over and roll out the rim on a Cel board, using a thin Cel stick. This will form the hip and calyx of the flower.

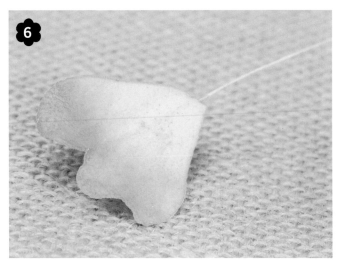

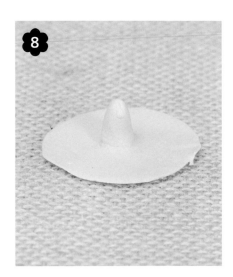

9 Place a medium-sized calyx cutter over the hip and cut out the calyx. Place the calyx on a foam pad. Using a small metal ball tool, thin out each sepal, balling each from the tip to the centre so that it curves inwards. Using a pair of fine scissors, cut into the sides of four of the sepals to form hairs.

10 Apply a thin layer of edible glue to the underside of the calyx, then thread the rose through the centre of the calyx and hip. Adjust the calyx so that it fits neatly on the back of the flower. Allow to partially dry before carefully dusting the hip and the sepals with hunter green dusting powder. Repeat steps 7–10 for the second flower.

Leaves

11 Roll out a size 10 (Sugarfacts guide) piece of pale green flower paste over the groove of a lightly greased Cel board. Cut out a series of leaves for each flower: you will need one large, two medium and two small leaves to make each leaf spray.

12 Insert a quarter-length of 30# white wire into the base and ridge on the back of each leaf. Vein each leaf with a rose leaf veiner and thin the edges with a metal ball tool, working half on the edge of the leaf and half on the foam pad. Allow to partially dry before dusting the top surface of the leaf with hunter green dusting powder. Spray the leaves with an edible glaze in a well-ventilated room.

13 Attach a half-length of 24# white wire to the base of the large leaf with half-width Nile green flower tape. Tape down the wire for 1in (2.5cm), then tape in two medium leaves on either side of the stem. Tape down a further 1in (2.5cm), then tape in the remaining two small leaves on either side of the stem. Bend the stem to give movement to it. Make three leaf sprays.

Rose hip

14 Roll a size 8 (Sugarfacts guide) piece of red flower paste into an egg shape. Make a small hook in the end of half a length of 24# white wire, then insert it into the thin end of the hip. Pull the wire down so that the hook embeds itself into the paste. Use a ball tool to make a hollow in the top of the hip. Allow to dry. Spray the surface of the bud with edible glaze spray in a well-ventilated room.

15 Roll out a size 6 (Sugarfacts guide) piece of toffee-coloured flower paste on a lightly greased Cel board. Use the small calyx cutter to cut out a calyx. Place the calyx on a foam pad and thin the edges of the sepals with a ball tool, applying pressure so that they curve inwards. Glue the calyx in place on top of the rose hip. Allow to partially dry before painting the centre of the calyx with liquorice black paste colour.

Flower spray assembly

16 Attach a length of half-width Nile green flower tape to the stem of a rose and tape in a spray of leaves above and behind the rose. Tape down for a further 1in (2.5cm) on the stem, then tape in the second rose. Attach a length of the green flower tape to the stem of the rose hip and tape in a leaf spray behind and to the right of the hip. Attach this spray to the stem of roses at the same point on the stem. Then tape in the third leaf spray at the same point on the left-hand side. Tape down the stem for a further ½in (1.25cm) to secure all the stems. Pass the finished spray quickly through a jet of steam to set the dusting powders onto the surface of the paste.

Gladiolus

This striking flower is sometimes known as the sword lily because of the sword-like strong green leaves that accompany the flowering spike. Gladioli come in a wide variety of colours and can vary in shape and size depending on type. They were introduced worldwide from South Africa in the seventeenth century. The small gladioli are popular in bridal work, as the flowers are dainty and often feature interesting splashes of colour.

Materials and Equipment

White flower paste

Pale green flower paste coloured with fern droplet liquid colour (Sugarflair)

30#, 28#, 26# and 24# white Sunrise wires (The Old Bakery)

Half-width Nile green flower tape (Hamilworth)

Rose campion dusting powder (Diamond)

Vine green dusting powder (Squires Kitchen)

Ginko and African violet dusting powders (EdAble Art)

Gladiolus sheath template (see page 145)

Gladiolus leaf template (see page 144)

Gladioli petal cutters 303 (Fine Cut Sugarcraft Products)

Stargazer B petal veiner (Squires Kitchen)

Amaryllis petal veiner, for leaf (Squires Kitchen)

Edible glue (homemade from tylose powder; see page 12)

Sugarcraft tools (see pages 14–17)

Method

Stamens

1 Attach a pea-sized/size 5 (Sugarfacts guide) piece of well-kneaded white flower paste to half a length of 30# white wire. Work the paste down the wire to cover about 2in (5cm) with a thin layer of flower paste. Flatten the tip to form the stamen. Dust the stamen with rose campion dusting powder on the tip and vine green dusting powder on the base. Bend the stamen into a gentle curve. Make three stamens.

Pistil

2 Repeat the process of making the stamen, but this time cut the tip into three, making two cuts with a pair of fine scissors. Bend the pistil to match the curve of the stamens. As before, dust with rose campion and vine green dusting powders.

Stamen/pistil assembly

3 Arrange the stamens side by side. Place the pistil at the back and slightly higher than the stamens. Tape together at the base with quarter-width Nile green flower tape (half-width tape cut into two with a tape shredder or scissors), stretching the tape to form a neat assembly. Attach a small ball of pale green flower paste to the base of the assembly and flatten it with your fingers.

Flower tepals

As the petals and sepals in this flower are very similar, they are known as tepals.

4 Roll a size 11 (Sugarfacts guide) piece of white flower paste into a sausage shape. Place over the groove of a lightly greased Cel board, and roll out the paste thinly along the groove using a non-stick rolling pin. Cut out the small tepal using the smaller gladioli petal cutter. Insert half a length of 28# white wire into the ridge on the back of the tepal.

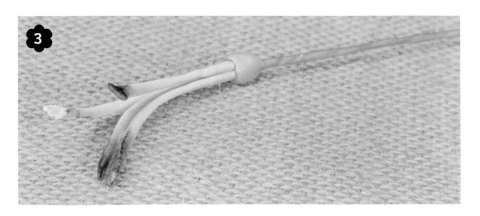

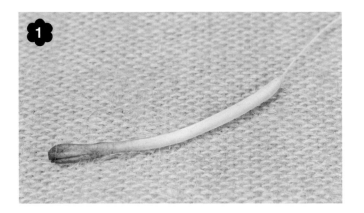

5 Vein the tepal with a Stargazer B lily petal veiner, applying pressure with your fingers to achieve good veining. Repeat steps 4 and 5 to make three tepals for the flower.

6 Soften the edges of the tepals using a ball tool on a foam pad, working half on the edge and half on the foam pad. This will thin and flute the edges.

7 Bend each tepal backwards in a soft curve to give them shape and form. Dust the edges with rose campion dusting powder, using a large chisel-shaped brush. Dust the base of the tepal with vine green dusting powder.

Tip

For a purple flower, dust the stamens and tepals with African violet dusting powder.

8 Attach a length of half-width Nile green flower tape to the base of the stamen/pistil assembly, then tape in the three small tepals to form a triangle. Allow to partially dry.

9 Cut out three more tepals using the large gladioli petal cutter. Repeat steps 4–7 with each of the larger tepals.

10 Attach a length of half-width Nile green flower tape to the base of the first row of tepals, then tape in the large tepals immediately underneath and in between the tepals of the first row. Dust the base of the flower with vine green dusting powder.

Sheath

11 A gladiolus flower does not have a calyx; it has a pale green sheath. Roll out a piece of pale green flower paste on a lightly greased Cel board, using a non-stick rolling pin. Vein this with an amaryllis petal veiner. Cut out two sheaths using the template on page 145.

12 Place the paste on a foam pad and thin the edges with a ball tool, taking care not to frill the edges. Apply a thin layer of edible glue to the back of each sheath. Place the first sheath on the right-hand side of the base of the flower, ensuring that it is attached to the tepal. Place the second sheath on the left-hand side of the base of the flower so that it overlaps the first sheath at the base and is attached to the tepals. Dust with vine green dusting powder using a chisel-shaped brush, taking some of the colour onto the base of the flower.

Flower bud

13 Roll a size 4 (Sugarfacts guide) ball of well-kneaded white flower paste into a long, thin cone shape. Insert half a length of 24# white wire into the base of the cone. Thin the paste on the wire and leave to dry.

14 Cut out three small tepals using the small gladioli petal cutter. Soften the edges on a foam pad and vein as for the flower. Apply a thin layer of edible glue to the edges of each tepal before attaching them in turn to the cone so that they spiral around each other. Pinch the base of the tepals onto the wire.

15 Dust the edges with rose campion dusting powder and the base with vine green dusting powder. Make and attach a sheath, as in steps 11–12. Dust with vine green dusting powder.

Looped leaves

Real gladioli leaves are long and sword-like in appearance. They are too large to be used in arrangements. I therefore chose to make the foliage as looped leaves, using the template on page 144.

16 Roll out a size 11 (Sugarfacts guide) ball of well-kneaded pale green flower paste into a sausage shape. Insert a full-length piece of 26# white wire into the centre of the paste so that the sausage is in the centre of the wire.

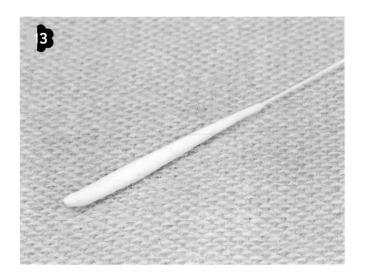

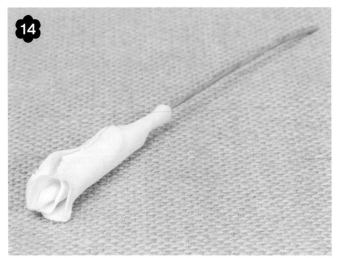

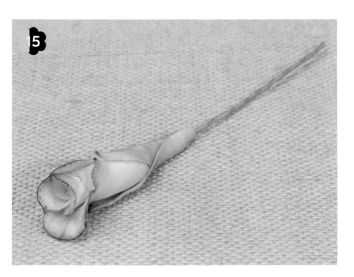

17 Flatten the paste around the wire using your fingers. Place on a lightly greased Cel board. Roll the paste out along the length of the wire, taking care not to apply too much pressure on the wire itself. Roll out the paste again on each side of the wire.

18 Place the gladiolus leaf template over the paste so that the wire runs down the centre of the template. Cut out the leaf shape using a wheel tool.

19 Place the wired leaf in the centre of an amaryllis petal veiner. Apply pressure to the veiner with your fingers so that the leaf has well-defined veins. Place the veined leaf on a foam pad and thin the edges by working half on the edge of the leaf and half on the foam pad with a ball tool.

20 Bend the centre of the leaf over so that the top and bottom of the leaf are level. Tape the two wires together using half-width Nile green flower tape. Adjust the finished depth of the leaf by closing the wires together. Allow to partially dry.

21 Dust the top surface of the leaf with ginko dusting powder with a chisel-shaped brush, working from the outside edge to the centre. Pass the partially dry leaf quickly through a jet of steam to set the colour onto the paste.

Assembly

22 Attach a length of half-width Nile green flower tape 1½in (4cm) from the base of the bud. Tape in the flower below and to the right of the bud, stretching the tape to secure the flower onto the stem. Add a looped leaf behind and to the left of the bud, taping at the same place. Tape down the stem for 1in (2.5cm) to complete the flower spray.

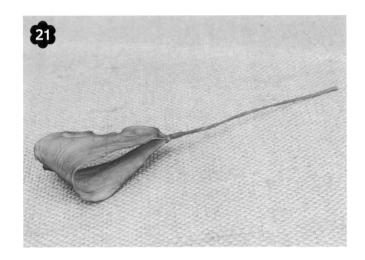

Japanese Anemone

Japanese anemone flowers can be single or double and emerge from tight, round buds on the tips of long stems. The single variety consists of six to eight white or pink petals around a green centre surrounded by yellow stamens. The double variety has at least nine petals in two rows. The pink variety used for the arrangement on page 134 is made in the same way as the white version (shown here), but dusted with pink and lavender powders.

Materials and Equipment

Pale green flower paste coloured with fern droplet liquid colour (Sugarflair)

White flower paste

K24 cream stamens (The Old Bakery)

30# and 24# white Sunrise wires (The Old Bakery)

Half-width white and Nile green flower tapes (Hamilworth)

Vine green dusting powder (Squires Kitchen)

Egg yellow dusting powder (Sugarflair)

Baby maize and aubergine dusting powders (EdAble Art)

Autumn green dusting powder (Rainbow Dust)

Rose petal cutters set 5802 (Fine Cut Sugarcraft Products)

Abutilon leaf cutters set 3 (Jem)

Camellia petal veiner (Squires Kitchen)

Aquilegia or hop leaf veiner (Squires Kitchen)

Sugarcraft tools (see pages 14–17)

Method

Centre

1 Roll out a size 6 (Sugarfacts guide) piece of pale green flower paste into a ball. Make a small hook on the end of half a length of 24# white wire and insert it into the top of the ball. Pull the wire down and secure the paste onto the wire by pinching the paste at the base.

2 Hold a pair of fine scissors vertically and cut into the surface of the paste to achieve a rough texture. Dust the top surface with vine green dusting powder using a chisel-shaped brush, working from the outside edge to the centre.

Stamens

3 Take 12 stamens, double them over and attach them to half a length of 30# white wire with half-width white flower tape, stretching the tape as you work to make a neat join. Paint the stamens with egg yellow dusting powder dissolved in water, using a small paintbrush. Make four groups of stamens.

Stamen/centre assembly

4 Attach a length of half-width Nile green flower tape to the base of the centre. Tape in the four stamen assemblies evenly around the centre, stretching the tape as you work so that the finished assembly is neat. Tape down the stem with the green flower tape.

Petals

Make nine wired petals for the double flower and six wired petals for the single version.

5 Roll out a size 10 (Sugarfacts guide) ball of white flower paste thinly over the groove of a lightly greased Cel board. Remove the paste from the board and turn the paste over so that the ridge is visible. Using the middle size rose petal cutter, cut out nine petals, with the ridge running down the centre of each petal. Insert a half-length of 30# white wire into the base of the each petal, pushing and twisting the wire up the ridge.

6 Vein each petal with a camellia petal veiner, pressing down firmly to achieve good veining. Soften the edges of the petal using a ball tool on a foam pad, working half on the petal edge and half on the pad. Dust the base of the petal with baby maize dusting powder.

Flower assembly

7 Attach a length of half-width Nile green flower tape to the base of the centre. Tape in six petals evenly around the centre, stretching the tape as you work. Tape down the wire to form the stem of the flower. (This is the single flower.)

8 Make another flower with a row of three petals taped in under the centre, followed by a second row of six petals taped in immediately underneath the first row. (This is the double flower.)

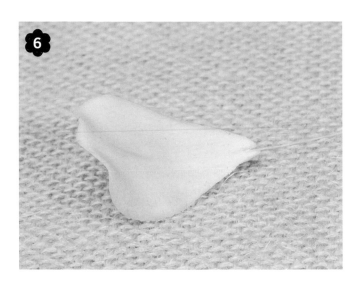

Leaves

9 Roll out a size 10 (Sugarfacts guide) ball of pale green flower paste over the groove of a lightly greased Cel board. Remove the paste from the board and cut out one large and two small leaves for each stem of leaves, using the abutilon leaf cutters. Insert a quarter-length of 30# white wire into the base of each leaf, pushing and twisting the wire up the ridge so that the leaf is fully wired.

10 Vein the leaves with an aquilegia or a hop leaf veiner. Soften the edges as before. Dust the top surface of the leaf with autumn green dusting powder and the underside of the leaves with aubergine dusting powder, using a chisel-shaped brush.

Leaf stem

11 Tape down the stem of each leaf for ½in (1.25cm) with quarter-width Nile green flower tape (half-width tape cut into two with a tape shredder or scissors). Take a large leaf and add two small leaves on either side of the stem of the large leaf. Insert half a length of 24# white wire here and tape down the wires to form a stem. Make three.

Buds

12 Roll out a size 6 (Sugarfacts guide) piece of pale green flower paste into a ball. Insert half a length of 24# white wire into the top of the ball. Pull the wire down so that it is embedded into the paste.

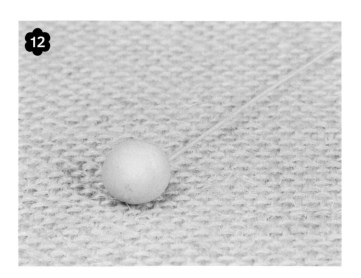

13 Mark several lines from the top to the base of the bud with a wheel tool. Dust the bud with autumn green dusting powder and the tip with aubergine dusting powder, using a chisel-shaped brush and working from the top of the bud to the base. Tape down the stem with half-width Nile green flower tape. Make two buds for each stem of flowers.

Flower spray

14 Attach a length of half-width Nile green flower tape 1in (2.5cm) below the leaves of a leaf spray. Insert two flower buds and tape onto the leaf stem using the green flower tape. Add a pair of leaves to the stem on either side of the buds.

15 Tape down the stem for 1½in (4cm) with half-width Nile green flower tape, stretching the tape as you work down the stem. Tape in the single Japanese anemone. Tape in a leaf spray using the green flower tape at this same point, followed by the double Japanese anemone. Attach a spray of leaves to the left and right of the final flower. Tape down the stem for ½in (1.25cm) to secure the assembly.

Old-Fashioned Double Rose

These fabulous roses are popular in bridal bouquets. The bloom style is diverse, with open cup, shallow cup, deep cup or rosettes; here I made the rosette form. To reduce the weight of the finished flower I used a polystyrene ball as a former, onto which I made the centre of the rose using a quilling technique to replicate the intricate centre petals. This is a David Austin type of rose, which provides both colour and fragrance in any garden or bridal bouquet.

Materials and Equipment

White flower paste

Pale green flower paste coloured with fern droplet liquid colour (Sugarflair)

28# and 24# white Sunrise wires (The Old Bakery)

Half-width Nile green flower tape (Hamilworth)

Carnation and hunter green dusting powders (Diamond)

Vine green dusting powder (Squires Kitchen)

Apple green dusting powder (Sugarflair)

Burgundy dusting powder (EdAble Art)

Rose petal cutters sets 582 and 583 (Fine Cut Sugarcraft Products)

Rose leaf cutter (Jem)

Calyx cutter 1½in (4cm) (Orchard Products)

Ribbon strip cutter (PME)

Rose petal veiner (Squires Kitchen)

Rose leaf veiner (Squires Kitchen)

Polystyrene ball 1½in (4cm) in diameter (Hobbycraft)

Edible glue (homemade from tylose powder; see page 12)

Sugarcraft tools (see pages 14–17)

Method

Centre

1 Cut the polystyrene ball into two with a sharp knife. Insert four half-lengths of 24# white wire into the ball from the bottom until they emerge at the top. Bend the end of each wire over and pull the hooked ends into the ball to secure.

2 Roll out a ball of white flower paste (or colour to match the flower) on a lightly greased non-stick board. Cut out a thin piece of flower paste the same size as the top of the ball and glue it in place over the wires with edible glue.

3 Roll out a ball of white flower paste thinly on a non-stick board. Using the ribbon strip cutter, cut out strips of paste ¼in (6mm) wide. Fold the strips into a teardrop shape with three to four layers. Make eight teardrop shapes.

4 Apply a thin layer of edible glue to the top of the ball and stick the eight teardrops in place, applying glue to the edges of each piece so that they stick together. Dust the tips of the centre with carnation dusting powder.

5 Roll out a ball of white flower paste on a lightly greased non-stick board. Cut out five rose petals, using the largest of the rose petal set 582 (measuring 1in/2.5cm across and 1½in/4cm long). Place the petal on a foam pad. Thin the edges and ball the centre of the petal with a ball tool. Dust the edges of the petal with carnation dusting powder and the base with vine green dusting powder.

6 Glue the five petals around the polystyrene ball so that the tops of the petals are in line with the centre.

7 Repeat steps 5–6 twice more, placing the second row of petals in between those of the first row and those of the third row in between those of the second row. Allow each row of petals to become a little more open.

8 Repeat steps 5–6 twice more, using a rose petal cutter 1½in (4cm) wide and 1¾in (4.5cm) long (the smallest of the rose petal set 583).

9 Roll out a ball of white flower paste over the groove of a Cel board. Cut out ten petals using the same cutter as for step 8. Insert half a length of 28# white wire into the base of each petal. Vein the petals with the rose petal veiner.

10 Place a petal on a foam pad. Thin the edges and ball the centre of each petal with a ball tool. Bend the wire in the petal. Dust the edges of the petal with carnation dusting powder and the base with vine green. Repeat this process for all ten petals.

11 Attach a length of half-width Nile green flower tape to the base of the rose underneath the petals. Tape in five of the wired petals evenly around the flower. Tape in the remaining five petals underneath this first layer. In between the petals of the previous rose, tape four half-lengths of 24# white wires to the stem for extra strength, using the green flower tape.

Calyx

12 Roll out a size 8 (Sugarfacts guide) piece of pale green flower paste into a fat cone. Insert the pointed end into the middle-sized hole of a foam pad and roll over the paste with a small Cel stick. Take the flattened cone out of the pad, turn it over and roll out the rim on a Cel board lightly dusted with cornflour, using a Cel stick. This will form both the hip and calyx of the flower.

13 Cut out a calyx using a 1½in (4cm) calyx cutter. Cut hairs into the edges of four of the sepals using a pair of fine scissors.

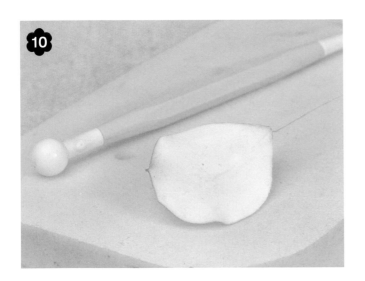

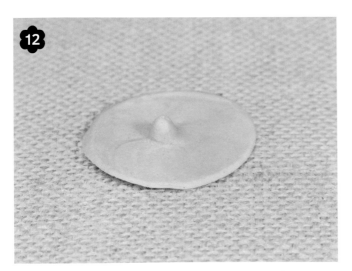

14 Apply a thin layer of edible glue to the flat surface of the calyx and pull the stem of the rose through the centre. Stick each sepal in place so that they fit neatly on the underside of the rose. Dust the surface of the calyx with hunter green dusting powder.

Bud

15 Roll out a size 10 (Sugarfacts guide) piece of white flower paste into a long cone. Insert half a length of 24# white wire into the base of the cone. Allow to partially dry for 30 minutes.

16 Repeat steps 12–13 to make the calyx of the rose bud.

17 Apply a thin layer of edible glue to the inside of the calyx. Insert the wired cone into the centre of the calyx and stick the sepals in place evenly around the cone. This forms the simple bud. Dust all over the surface of the bud with hunter green dusting powder, using a chisel-shaped brush. Tape in three half-lengths of 24# white wire to make the stem, using half-width Nile green flower tape.

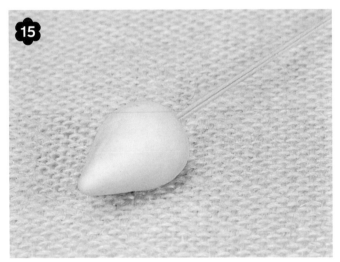

Leaves

The leaves on this rose are too large and long to be used with the flower. I adapted the stem of leaves by using just the top half, which is three large leaves taped together.

18 Roll out a ball of pale green flower paste over the groove of a lightly greased Cel board. Cut out three large leaves for each spray of leaves, using the rose leaf cutter.

19 Insert a quarter-length of 30# white wire into the base of each leaf, pushing the wire up the ridge on the back so that the leaf is fully wired. Vein the wired leaf with a rose leaf veiner and press down firmly to achieve good veining. Bend the wire to give movement to the leaf. Dust the leaf with apple green dusting powder, followed by hunter green in the centre and burgundy dusting powder on the leaf edge.

20 Attach a length of half-width Nile green flower tape to the base of the large leaf. Tape down the stem for 1in (2.5cm). Tape in the two remaining leaves on either side of the stem, adding a short length of 24# white wire here for extra strength. Tape down the stem to complete the leaf spray, stretching the tape as you work so that the stem is not bulky.

Flower spray

21 Attach a length of half-width Nile green flower tape halfway down the stem of the bud. Tape in a leaf spray so that it sits behind the bud. Tape down the stem to leave sufficient room for the rose to be added.

22 Add the rose to the stem and tape in firmly with half-width Nile green flower tape. Tape in a leaf spray onto the stem with the back of the leaves facing. Pull the leaf spray over towards you so that the leaves are now below the rose. Tape in another leaf spray on the other side of the stem. Pass the completed rose spray quickly through a jet of steam to set the dusting colours onto the surface of the paste.

Dahlia

These popular garden flowers provide spectacular displays in late summer and early autumn and as cut flowers for use in the home due to their magnificent colours. Dahlia flowers can be virtually any colour, through shades of white, yellow, orange, flame, red, pink, lilac or purple and even bi-colour mixes. There are several forms of dahlias; I chose to make the single dahlia. These have a single row of petals around a central disc and grow to 18in (45cm) tall.

Materials and Equipment

Yellow flower paste coloured with mimosa dusting powder (EdAble Art)

Orange flower paste coloured with orange dusting powder (Squires Kitchen)

Pale green flower paste coloured with fern droplet liquid colour (Sugarflair)

28# and 24# white Sunrise wires (The Old Bakery)

Half-width Nile green flower tape (Hamilworth)

Saffron dusting powder (EdAble Art)

Nasturtium dusting powder (Squires Kitchen)

Apple green dusting powder (Sugarflair)

Hunter green dusting powder (Diamond)

Australian rose petal cutters (Tinkertech Two) or dahlia petal template (see page 144)

Eight-pointed chrysanthemum cutter 1½in (4cm) (Jem)

Daisy centre mould/cutter from set 165 (Jem)

Small calyx cutter (Fine Cut Sugarcraft Products)

Dahlia leaf template (see page 144)

Camellia petal veiner (Squires Kitchen)

Hydrangea leaf veiner (Squires Kitchen)

Edible glue (homemade from tylose powder; see page 11)

Sugarcraft tools (see pages 14–17)

Method

Centre

1 Take a size 6 (Sugarfacts guide) piece of well-kneaded yellow flower paste and roll into a ball. Push the ball of paste into the second largest size of daisy mould. Remove the paste carefully from the mould and insert half a length of 24# white wire into the centre. Press the paste carefully onto the wire to secure the centre. Leave to dry for a few minutes.

2 Reshape the top with your fingers to hide where the wire has entered. Dust the surface of the centre with mimosa dusting powder and the edges with orange dusting powder, working carefully from the outside edge with a chisel-shaped brush.

Petals

3 Roll out a piece of well-kneaded orange flower paste thinly over the groove on a lightly greased grooved Cel board. Cut out seven petals using a 1½in (4cm) long Australian rose petal cutter or cut the petals out with a wheel tool using the dahlia petal template (see page 144). Insert half a length of 28# white wire into the base of each petal and push the wire up the ridge on the back of the petals.

4 Vein the wired petals with a camellia petal veiner. Press down firmly. Place the petals on a foam pad and thin the edges with a ball tool, working half on the petal edge and half on the foam pad.

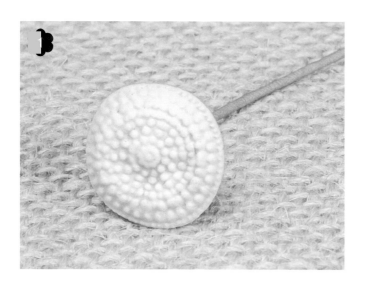

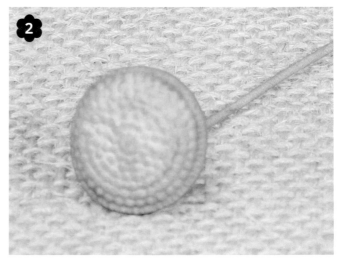

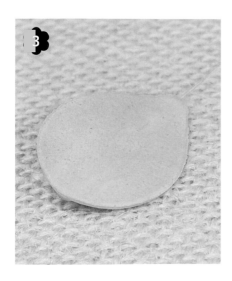

5 Bend the wire in the petals backwards to give them shape and allow them to dry on bumpy foam to maintain their shape.

6 Dust the petals all over with saffron dusting powder, followed by nasturtium dusting powder on the edges.

7 Attach a length of half-width Nile green flower tape to the underside of the centre of the flower. Tape in the first petal so that it sits underneath the centre. Tape in the remainder of the petals so that each one sits next to the previous petal. Rearrange the petals if necessary so that they fit neatly next to each other.

Calyx

Dahlia flowers have a double calyx.

8 To make the first layer, pinch out a size 8 (Sugarfacts guide) piece of pale green flower paste to form a shape like a sombrero.

9 Roll out the base thinly on a non-stick board with a thin Cel stick and cut out the calyx using the eight-pointed chrysanthemum cutter. Place the calyx on a non-stick board and use a small Cel stick to widen each sepal.

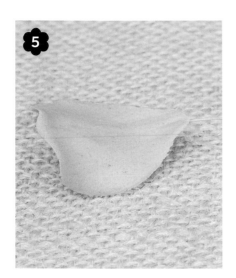

10 Make a hole in the centre of the calyx for the stem of the flower to pass through. Apply a thin layer of edible glue to the underside of the calyx. Pull the stem of the flower through the calyx and press the calyx onto the back of the flower. Cut away most of the paste at the back of the calyx to leave a stub of about ¼in (6mm). Flatten with a Dresden tool, then dust the calyx all over with apple green dusting powder.

11 To make the second layer, roll out a size 6 (Sugarfacts guide) piece of pale green flower paste on a lightly greased Cel board. Remove the paste from the board, dust the board with cornflour, then replace the green paste on the dusted surface and cut out a calyx using the small metal calyx cutter.

12 Place the calyx on the foam pad and use a small ball tool to pull down the paste from the tip to the centre to curl each sepal.

13 Carefully dust the calyx all over with apple green dusting powder. Apply a thin layer of edible glue to the calyx and pull the wired flower through the centre of the calyx and stick it onto the back of the stub of paste. Allow to dry.

Bud

14 Take a size 8 (Sugarfacts guide) piece of orange flower paste and roll it into a cone shape. Flatten the wide end with your fingers. Push four half-lengths of 24# white wires into the base of the bud (the thin end). Pinch the paste onto

the wire.Using a wheel tool, draw lines down the bud from top to bottom. Dust the bud with saffron dusting powder. Allow it to dry overnight.

15 Make a calyx in the same way as for the flower and glue it in place on the back of the bud.

Leaves

16 Roll out a size 12 (Sugarfacts guide) piece of pale green flower paste over the groove of a lightly greased large Cel board. Place the leaf template over the paste so that the groove runs down the centre of the leaf. Cut around the template with a wheel tool to cut out the leaf. Repeat this process to make three leaves.

17 Insert a quarter-length of 28# white wire into the base of the leaf, pushing and twisting the wire to the top. Vein the leaf with a hydrangea leaf veiner. Dust the front of the leaf with hunter green dusting powder. Allow to dry, then pass the leaf through a jet of steam from an electric steamer to set the dusting powder onto the surface of the leaf.

Flower assembly

18 Attach a length of half-width Nile green tape 2in (5cm) from the base of the bud. Tape in a leaf to the right-hand side of the stem of the bud.

19 Continue to tape down the stem, positioning the flower below the bud. Tape in the flower with half-width Nile green flower tape. Tape in two more leaves around the stem and below the flower.

Clematis

There are approximately 300 species of clematis found worldwide. There are many different forms and sizes, some as small as a ping-pong ball and some as large as a dinner plate. They are vigorous climbers. The number of petals varies from four to eight for the single varieties that I have made here. They come in white, cream and all shades of pink, lavender, purple and even red.

Materials and Equipment

Cream flower paste coloured with baby maize dusting powder (EdAble Art)

Lavender flower paste coloured with lavender dusting powder (EdAble Art)

Pale green flower paste coloured with fern droplet liquid colour (Sugarflair)

28# and 24# white Sunrise wires (The Old Bakery)

Half-width Nile green flower tape (Hamilworth)

Rose campion dusting powder (Diamond)

Myrtle dusting powder (Squires Kitchen)

Apple green dusting powder (Sugarflair)

Daisy plunger cutters, medium and large (PME)

Valotta lily petal cutter 699 (Fine Cut Sugarcraft Products)

Clematis leaf cutters 1872 (Fine Cut Sugarcraft Products)

Clematis petal veiner (Squires Kitchen)

Clematis leaf veiner (Squires Kitchen)

Edible glue (homemade from tylose powder; see page 12)

Sugarcraft tools (see pages 14–17)

Method

Centre

1 Roll a size 7 (Sugarfacts guide) piece of cream flower paste into a ball. Make a flat hook in the end of a half-length 24# white wire and insert it into the centre of the ball. Pull the wire down so that the hook is embedded in the paste.

2 Roll out a ball of cream flower paste on a lightly greased Cel board. Cut out a daisy with the medium-sized daisy plunger cutter. Place the cut-out daisy on a foam pad and thin each petal with a small ball tool.

3 Paint the daisy with edible glue. Insert the wired centre through the middle of the daisy and pull the petals up and into the centre of the ball so that it is completely covered. Allow to partially dry.

4 Repeat steps 2 and 3, leaving some of the petal ends free.

5 Roll out a ball of cream flower paste on a lightly greased Cel board. Cut out a daisy using the large daisy plunger cutter. Cut each petal into two with a wheel tool or scalpel. Attach to the centre with edible glue, allowing the petal ends to be free. Allow to partially dry before dusting the edges with lavender dusting powder.

Petals

6 Roll out a ball of lavender flower paste over the groove of a large Cel board. Cut out six petals using the Valotta lily petal cutter. Insert a half-length of 28# white wire into the base of each petal. Push and twist the wire up the ridge so that the petals are fully wired.

7 Vein the petals using a clematis petal veiner, pressing down hard on the top veiner to ensure strong veining of the petal. Then place the petals on a foam pad and thin the edges with a ball tool.

8 Place the petals on a non-stick board dusted with cornflour. Frill the edges with a small Cel stick.

9 Dust the base of the petals with rose campion dusting powder and the edges with lavender dusting powder. Bend the wires in the petals so that they curve gently backwards.

Flower assembly

10 Attach a length of half-width Nile green flower tape immediately underneath the centre. Tape in three petals evenly around the centre, using the green tape.

11 Tape in the remaining three petals in the gaps. Tape down the stem with green flower tape, stretching the tape as you work down the stem.

Bud

12 Roll a size 11 (Sugarfacts guide) piece of pale green flower paste into a fat cone shape. Insert four half-lengths of 24# white wire into the base, pinching the paste onto the wire. Mark the surface of the cone with fine lines from the tip to the base, using a wheel tool.

13 Dust the surface of the cone with myrtle dusting powder using a chisel-shaped brush, working from the tip of the bud to the base.

Leaves

The leaves vary in shape and form depending on the variety of clematis. I made leaves using the 1872 clematis leaf cutters.

14 Roll out a ball of pale green flower paste over the groove of a lightly greased Cel board. Remove the paste from the board, turn it over and cut out four small and four large leaves. Insert a quarter-length of 28# white wire into the base of each leaf, pushing and twisting the wire so that it reaches the top of the leaf.

15 Vein each leaf using a clematis leaf veiner. Place the veined leaves on a foam pad and thin the edges with a ball tool. Bend the wire within each leaf to give them movement.

16 Dust the top surface of each leaf with apple green dusting powder using a chisel-shaped brush, working from the outside edges to the centre.

Assembly

17 Attach a length of half-width Nile green flower tape to the end of a 24# white wire. Tape down the wire for 1in (2.5cm), then tape in a pair of the small leaves, one on each side of the stem. Tape for a further 1in (2.5cm) down the stem, then tape in another pair of small leaves on either side of the stem. Tape down the stem for a further 1in (2.5.cm), then tape in the bud and a pair of the large leaves. Tape down the stem for 3in (7.5cm) to allow room for the flower.

18 Position the flower underneath the leaf/bud stem, with 2in (5cm) of stem on the flower. Now tape the flower in with half-width Nile green flower tape, immediately followed by the remaining two large leaves positioned on either side of the stem. Pass the finished spray quickly though a jet of steam from an electric steamer to set the dusting powders onto the surface of the flower paste.

Hellebore

Flowering from late winter into early spring, hellebores come in a wide variety of colours. Many sugarcraft hellebores can be produced by using different-coloured centres combined with different-coloured bracts (petals). They can either be plain or have dots or veins painted on them. The leaves of these flowers are very large compared to the size of the flower. I have made much smaller leaves but of the same form to complement these lovely flowers.

Materials and Equipment

Burgundy flower paste (A Piece of Cake)

White flower paste

Pale green flower paste coloured with fern droplet liquid colour (Sugarflair)

K24 cream stamens (The Old Bakery)

30# and 26# white Sunrise wires (Old Bakery)

Half-width Nile green flower tape (Hamilworth)

Baby maize and dogwood red dusting powders (EdAble Art)

Vine green dusting powder (Squires Kitchen)

Rose campion and hunter green dusting powders (Diamond)

Hellebore leaf templates (see page 145)

Medium-sized calyx cutter set 165 (Fine Cut Sugarcraft Products)

Medium-sized Christmas rose petal cutter (Fine Cut Sugarcraft Products)

Christmas rose petal veiner (Squires Kitchen)

Hellebore leaf veiner (Squires Kitchen)

Edible glue (homemade from tylose powder; see page 11)

Sugarcraft tools (see pages 14–17)

Method

Stamen and nectary assembly

1 Take 15 stamens and double them over to give 30 stamen heads. Place four half-length 26# white wires evenly around the stamens and projecting above the stamen heads for ¼in (6mm). Attach a length of half-width Nile green flower tape ½in (1.25cm) below the stamen heads.

2 Pull the wires down in turn and tape down over the wires to form the stem of the flower. Dust the stamens with baby maize dusting powder.

3 Roll out a size 12 (Sugarfacts guide) piece of burgundy flower paste on a lightly greased non-stick board. Cut out two shapes for the nectary using the calyx cutter. Thin the sepals of the calyx with a ball tool, working on a foam pad. Stroke the end of each sepal inwards. Apply a thin layer of edible glue to the inside of the sepals. Glue the end of the sepal into the middle of the calyx. This is the nectary. Make two.

4 Apply a dot of glue to the centre of one of the nectaries. Glue both together.

5 Insert the stamen assembly into the centre of the nectary, pushing it into place and pinching at the base to fit snugly around and under the stamens.

Petals (coloured bracts)

6 Roll out a piece of white flower paste thinly over the groove of a lightly greased Cel board. Cut out five petals, using the Christmas rose petal cutter. Insert a length of 30# white wire into the base of the ridge on the back of each petal.

7 Vein the wired petals with a Christmas rose petal veiner, then place the petals on a foam pad and thin the edges with a ball tool, working half on the edge of each petal and half on the foam pad.

8 Support the petals in your hand while you bend the wire inside them so that each petal is curved.

9 Dust the base of each petal with vine green dusting powder. Dust the edges of each petal, first with rose campion dusting powder and then with dogwood dusting powder, using a chisel-shaped brush and working from the outside edge inwards. Paint in lines on each petal, using dogwood dusting powder dissolved in alcohol or water.

10 Attach three petals to the base of the stamen/nectary in a triangular arrangement, with half-width Nile green flower tape, then tape in the two remaining petals in the gaps. Adjust the petals to give a pleasing and natural shape.

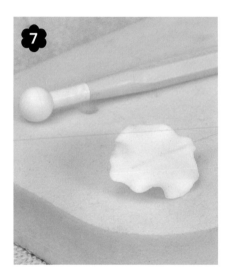

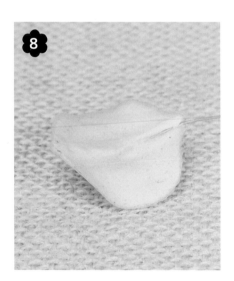

Flower bud

11 Take a size 8 (Sugarfacts guide) piece of white flower paste, form it into a cone shape, and insert four 26# wires into the base. Mark the top of the bud into three using a wheel tool. Dust the top of the bud with dogwood red dusting powder and the base with vine green dusting powder. Tape down the stem using half-width Nile green flower tape.

Leaves

12 Thinly roll out a ball of size 13 (Sugarfacts guide) pale green flower paste on a lightly greased Cel board. Using the Hellebore leaf templates on page 145, cut out four small and three large leaves.

13 Insert a one-third length of 30# white wire into the base and up into the ridge of each leaf. Vein each wired leaf with a hellebore leaf veiner, pressing down firmly to give good veining. Place the wired, veined leaves on a foam pad and soften the edges using a ball tool, working half on the leaf edge and half on the foam pad to produce a soft, fluted effect. Bend the wire in each leaf to give movement, then allow them to partially dry.

14 Dust each leaf on the front only with hunter green dusting powder, using a chisel-shaped brush. Carefully dust the edges with dogwood red dusting powder, working from the outside edge to the centre on both sides of each leaf. Allow to dry.

Leaf assembly

15 Attach a length of half-width Nile green flower tape to one of the large-sized leaves, then tape in two more large leaves side by side and next to the first leaf. Tape in a small leaf on either side of these three leaves. Tape down the stem with half-width Nile green flower tape to form the stem.

Flower assembly

16 Attach the remaining two small leaves to the base of the bud using half-width Nile green flower tape. Continue to tape down the stem, stretching the tape as you work so that there is a thin layer of tape on the stem.

17 Attach a length of half-width Nile green flower tape 2in (5cm) down the stem of the bud. Tape in the flower. Place the leaf assembly immediately underneath the flower and tape in the leaves with the flower tape.

Foliage

Laurustinus

This attractive winter-flowering evergreen shrub has dark green foliage and white or pale pink flowers. The buds open into tiny star-shaped flowers on flattened heads; these are followed by small blue-black berries. The berries tend to remain on the plant all year and do not appear to be eaten by birds. I have chosen to make the pink variety and used this foliage flower in the arrangements that are featured on pages 136 and 142.

Materials and Equipment

White flower paste

Pale green flower paste coloured with fern droplet liquid colour (Sugarflair)

Navy blue flower paste (Squires Kitchen)

Small micro white stamens KM05 (The Old Bakery)

30#, 28# and 24# white Sunrise wires (The Old Bakery)

26# beige wires (Hamilworth)

Half-width white and beige flower tapes (Hamilworth)

Vine green dusting powder (Squires Kitchen)

Carnation, ivy and hunter green dusting powders (Diamond)

Navy blue and blackberry dusting powders (EdAble Art)

Laurustinus leaf templates (see page 145)

Small blossom cutter 180 (Fine Cut)

Gardenia leaf veiner (Squires Kitchen)

Edible spray glaze (PME)

Sugarcraft tools (see pages 14–17)

Method

Wire cage

1 Take three half-length 28# white wires, fold in half and twist the wires together near one end to give six wires joined together. Cut out one wire with a pair of wire cutters – this forms a five-wire cage. Open up the wires slightly so that you will be able to insert a small bud into the top of the cage.

Buds

2 Take a tiny piece of white flower paste and form it into a cone shape. Insert a quarter-length piece of 30# white wire into the pointed end of the cone. Rub the base of the bud onto the wire. Insert the top of the bud into the cage. Press the wires onto the bud. This will divide the top of the bud into five to resemble an opening flower. Dust the base of each bud with vine green dusting powder, and the tips with carnation dusting powder.

3 Make 25 buds for each flower spray (50 in total), cutting out at least half of the wires about 1in (2.5cm) below the base of the buds. This will make a narrower stem. Insert four half-lengths of 24# white wires into the centre of the bunch and tape at the base with quarter-width white flower tape (half-width tape cut into two with a tape shredder or scissors). Stretch the tape as you work down the stem to give a neater finish.

Flower stamens

4 Fold three tiny stamens into two to give six heads. Remove one with a pair of scissors. Place a 30# white wire alongside and slightly above the stamens. Attach a length of quarter-width white flower tape to the base of the stamens and tape firmly together. Pull the wire down over the tape and tape over with the white tape to form a neat assembly.

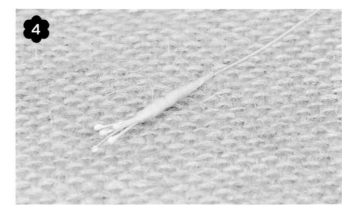

5 Take a small ball of white flower paste and roll it into a cone shape. Insert it into the small hole of a foam pad and roll over the paste with a small Cel stick. Take the flattened cone out of the pad, place it on a Cel board and roll out the rim with the Cel stick. Flatten the cone shape with your fingers and roll this out with a small Cel rolling pin to give a thin-rimmed sombrero shape.

6 Remove from the foam pad, place on a non-stick board and cut out a flower using the small blossom cutter placed over the centre of the sombrero shape. Thin and shape each petal using a tiny ball tool.

7 Insert the pointed end of a thin Cel stick into the centre of each flower. Open up slightly and insert the stamen assembly. Reshape the back of the tiny flower, removing any excess paste with your fingers. Dust as before for the buds.

8 Attach five to seven flowers around the tight bunch of buds with quarter-width white tape. Insert four 24# white wires into the base of the buds and tape down with quarter-width beige flower tape to form the stem.

Leaves

9 Roll out a ball of pale green flower paste over the groove on a lightly greased Cel board with a non-stick rolling pin. Cut out two small and two large leaves for each flower stem and two large leaves for each berry stem, using a wheel tool and the leaf templates (see page 145), making sure that the ridge runs down the centre of each leaf.

10 Insert a quarter-length of 30# white wire into the ridge on the back of each leaf. Soften the edges of the leaves with a ball tool on a foam pad, working half on the leaf edge and half on the foam pad.

11 Vein each wired leaf with a gardenia leaf veiner, pressing down firmly with your fingers to achieve good veining. Bend the wire in the leaves backwards to give a natural and pleasing shape. Allow them to partially dry, then dust the top surface with a mixture of ivy and hunter green dusting powders, using a chisel-shaped brush and working from the outside edge to the centre.

12 Using quarter-width white flower tape, attach a pair of small leaves just below the flower spray. Tape down ½in (1.25cm) and tape in a pair of large leaves opposite the first pair.

Berries

13 Take a size 4 (Sugarfacts guide) piece of well-kneaded navy blue flower paste and roll it into a small cone shape. Insert a quarter-length piece of 26# beige wire into the rounded

end of the berry. Roll the paste between your fingers to push the paste onto the wire to produce a pointed berry.

14 Dust the berries with a mixture of navy blue and blackberry dusting powders. Pass the berries through a jet of steam from an electric steamer to set the dusting powders onto the paste. When dry, spray each berry with edible spray glaze in a well-ventilated room or outside. Make 12–15 berries for each spray.

15 Tape 12–15 berries together with half-width beige flower tape, adding four 24# wires into the bunch to strengthen the stem. At the same time, cut out at least half of the berry stems with wire cutters to give a neater, narrower stem.

16 Attach a pair of large leaves in the same manner as for the flower stem. Steam the spray briefly to set the dusting powders onto the surface of the flower paste.

Arrangement of buds, flowers and berries

17 Tape two sprays of buds/flowers together with half-width beige flower tape. At this point on the stem, tape in two large leaves on either side of the stem. Tape down the stem for 1in (2.5cm), then tape in a spray of berries and leaves. Tape down the stem to cover all the wires with the beige tape. Adjust the flower, leaves and berries with a pair of angled tweezers to achieve an attractive spray.

Italian Arum

This is a ground-cover plant that grows in the spring. The leaves can vary in size from 2in (5cm) up to 6in (15cm) and are dark green with paler green markings. I have recreated this marking by painting with a mixture of hunter green and nutkin brown dusting powders dissolved in a solution of gum arabic, using a size 3 sable brush. I have used different sizes of this leaf in several arrangements in this book.

Materials and Equipment

Pale green flower paste coloured with fern droplet liquid colour (Sugarflair)

26# white Sunrise wire (The Old Bakery)

Hunter green dusting powder (Diamond)

Nutkin brown dusting powder (Squires Kitchen)

Gum arabic

Italian arum leaf template (see page 144)

Arum lily leaf veiner (Squires Kitchen)

Sugarcraft tools (see pages 14–17)

Method

Leaves

1 Roll out a sausage of pale green flower paste, then insert half a length of 26# white wire into the centre of the paste.

2 Flatten the paste around the wire with your fingers, then place it on a non-stick board. Roll the paste out sideways in both directions to thin it away from the wire, so that it's thickest around the wire. Place the arum lily leaf template (see page 144) centrally over the paste and cut out the leaf shape using a wheel tool.

3 Vein the leaf with an arum lily leaf veiner. Place the leaf on a foam pad and thin the edges by applying pressure to the edge with a ball tool.

4 Bend the wire so that the leaf has a natural shape. Pinch the paste around the wire on the back of the leaf to give further movement. Allow to partially dry for 30 minutes.

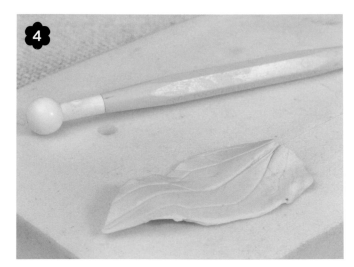

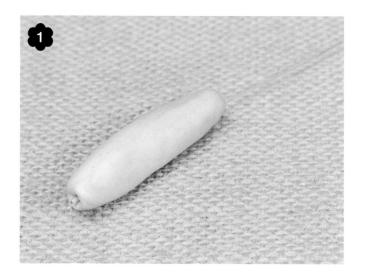

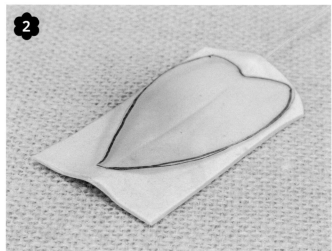

5 Using a mixture of hunter green and nutkin brown dusting powders mixed with a solution of gum arabic, paint in the details of the leaf following the pattern given, or use a real leaf for guidance.

Tip

Allow 30 minutes for the gum arabic to disperse into the water to make a solution. Use a size 3 brush for painting leaves of this size. Always wash the colour out from the brush under cold running water until the water runs clear. Allow the brush to fully dry before you put it away.

Ground Ivy

This perennial form of ivy grows wild in hedgerows. It is notable for its clusters of delicate flowers followed by long-lasting berries first produced in winter. These berries are a paler green at first, then age to almost black, and are popular with flower arrangers, particularly at Christmastime in Europe. The leaves are shiny and dark green. The leaves and berries are borne on a twig-coloured stem. I have used this foliage in the arrangement on page 128.

Materials and Equipment

Pale green flower paste coloured with fern droplet liquid colour (Sugarflair)

28# and 24# white and 28# dark green Sunrise wires (The Old Bakery)

Half-width beige flower tape (Hamilworth)

Autumn green dusting powder (EdAble Art)

Ivy dusting powder (Diamond)

Bulrush brown dusting powder (Squires Kitchen)

Ground ivy leaf templates (see page 144)

Large gardenia leaf veiner (Squires Kitchen)

Sugarcraft tools (see pages 14–17)

Method

Berries

1 Take a size 4 (Sugarfacts guide) piece of pale green flower paste. Roll it into a ball and insert a third of a length of 28# dark green wire into the ball until it just pushes through the top surface of the berry and is visible.

2 Pinch the base of the berry to secure the berry onto the wire. Allow to dry for 30 minutes, then dust the berries with a mixture of autumn green and ivy dusting powders followed by bulrush dusting powder, using a chisel-shaped brush and working from the top of the berry to the base.

3 Pass the berry quickly through a jet of steam to set the dusting powder on the berry. Tape several berries together onto half a length of 24# white wire to form a stem.

Leaves

4 Roll out a piece of pale green flower paste over the groove of a lightly greased Cel board. Place the templates (see page 144) over the paste so that the groove runs down the centre of the leaf template. Cut round the template with a wheel tool. Cut out two small and three large leaves.

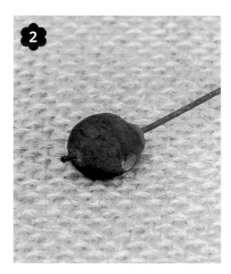

5 Insert a third of a length of white 28# wire into the ridge at the back of each leaf, pushing and twisting the wire up so that each leaf is completely wired. Vein the wired leaves using a large gardenia leaf veiner, pressing down firmly to achieve good veining.

6 Soften the edges of the leaves by placing them on a foam pad and applying pressure with a ball tool, working half on the leaf edge and half on the pad. Dust all over the front of each leaf with ivy dusting powder using a chisel-shaped brush, then dust bulrush brown in the centres.

7 Attach the leaves to the stem of berries with half-width beige flower tape. Dust the tape with bulrush brown dusting powder to resemble a twig. Pass the completed stem through a jet of steam to set the dusting powders onto the surface of the paste.

Variegated Ivy

This attractive foliage generally has small leaves, often with a green centre and cream or yellow margin to the leaf, or with a cream centre and green margin. Because of its trailing habit, this foliage is often used in wedding arrangements, either trailing around tables or as trailing foliage in bridal bouquets. Variegated ivy is ideal as an accompaniment to sugar flowers; I have used it in the arrangements on pages 128 and 136.

Materials and Equipment

Cream flower paste coloured with baby maize dusting powder (EdAble Art)

28# and 24# white Sunrise wires (Old Bakery)

Half-width beige flower tape (Hamilworth)

Euphorbia green dusting powder (EdAble Art)

White dusting powder (Sugarflair)

Ivy leaf cutters sets 375, 380 and 385 (Fine Cut Sugarcraft Products)

Ivy leaf veiner (Squires Kitchen)

Sugarcraft tools (see pages 14–17)

Method

Leaves

1 Roll out a size 12 (Sugarfacts guide) piece of cream flower paste over the groove of a lightly greased Cel board. Using the ivy leaf cutter sets, cut out two small, two medium and one large ivy leaf.

2 Insert a one-third length of 28# white wire into the base of each leaf and push it up the ridge at the back so that the leaf is supported on the wire.

3 Vein each wired leaf one at a time, pushing down firmly to achieve good veining. Place the veined leaves on a foam pad and thin the edges using a ball tool, working half on the leaf edge and half on the foam pad. Give movement to the leaves by running your fingers up the back on either side of the wire, then bend the wire backwards to give further shape to the leaves.

4 Dust the centre of each leaf with euphorbia green dusting powder, taking care to leave a cream edge. Paint in small white dots, using white dusting powder dissolved in water or clear alcohol.

5 Attach a small leaf to a length of 24# white wire and tape the leaf onto this wire with half-width beige flower tape. Tape down the stem for about 1in (2.5cm), then tape in the next leaf of the same size. Repeat this process, adding the larger leaves. Pass the finished stem of leaves through a jet of steam to set the powders onto the surface of the paste.

Tip

You can make different colours of ivy – for example, a dark green variety or one with green/brown leaves – using the same cutters and technique. They can then be dusted with appropriate colours. Look in hedgerows or at plants in garden centres, and take photos so you can replicate the colours.

Aquilegia Seed Heads

Aquilegia plants flower during the summer months. I love the seed heads that the flowers produce; these are usually green, although some have purple tips. If left on the plant, they dry out in autumn, turn brown and release their seeds to produce new plants for the following season. Aquilegia seed heads are easy to make and add texture and interest to flower sprays and arrangements. I have used them in the arrangements on pages 132, 136 and 142.

Materials and Equipment

Pale green flower paste coloured with fern droplet liquid colour (Sugarflair)

28# white Sunrise wires (The Old Bakery)

Half-width white flower tape (Hamilworth)

Vine green dusting powder (Squires Kitchen)

Aubergine dusting powder (EdAble Art)

Sugarcraft tools (see pages 14–17)

Method

Seed heads

1 Roll out 11 size 3 (Sugarfacts guide) pieces of pale green flower paste into balls, then into cone shapes.

2 Insert a half-length of 28# white wire into the fat end of each cone shape, pinching the paste at the base onto the wire. Dust the surface of the seed heads with vine green dusting powder and the tips with aubergine dusting powder.

3 Attach a length of quarter-width white flower tape (half-width tape cut into two with a tape shredder or scissors) to the base of one of the cone-shaped seed heads, add two cones next to the first one, and tape all three together tightly so that the seed heads stick together. Make two, then make a stem with five cones.

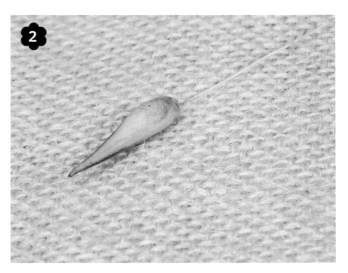

4 Attach a length of quarter-width white flower tape 2in (5cm) below the base of a three-cone seed head. Add a stem with two seed heads, followed by a stem with five seed heads at this point, and tape down the stem to cover all of the wires. Dust the stem on one side with vine green dusting powder and the other side with aubergine dusting powder. Pass the finished spray of aquilegia seed heads quickly through a jet of steam from an electric steamer to set the dusting powders onto the surface of the flower paste.

Tip
Aquilegia seed heads are quick and easy to make, so they could be produced from any leftover pale green flower paste and stored in a cardboard box until required. They make excellent fillers to add interest and texture to flower sprays or arrangements. Try making some with beige-coloured flower paste for use in autumnal floral pieces.

Floral Arrangements

Camellia Spray

This striking display of deep pink camellias is complemented by foliage that is available at the time the camellia flowers: variegated ivy, ground ivy and Italian arum leaves. The ground ivy berries add another element of structure alongside the delicate blooms. This bright and abundant arrangement makes a simply stunning birthday celebration cake.

Materials and Equipment

3 deep pink camellias (see page 30)

3 camellia leaves (see page 30)

4 ground ivy sprays (see page 114)

4 sprays of variegated ivy comprising 1 small, 2 medium and 1 large leaf (see page 118)

3 Italian arum leaves (see page 110)

Half-width Nile green flower tape (Hamilworth)

Large posy pick

5in (7.5cm) sugarpasted cake

Method

Attach a leaf to the right-hand side of each camellia and a variegated ivy leaf spray behind each flower with flower tape. Make three sprays.

Tape together a spray of ground ivy and a spray of variegated ivy.

Tape down the stem, then tape in each camellia flower/leaf spray individually below the ground ivy and variegated ivy.

Tape a spray of ground ivy leaves and berries in between each flower.

Finish the arrangement with three Italian arum leaves positioned and taped in under each camellia.

Place the finished spray into a posy pick that has been inserted into the centre of the cake.

Mixed Wild Flowers

A delighfully simple combined spray of wild poppy, foxglove, honeysuckle and wild rose makes the perfect arrangement for beginners looking to gain confidence in producing neat floral sprays. The contrasting colours provide all the drama that this beautifully effective arrangement needs. It would look very pretty placed delicately around the tiers of a country-style wedding cake, perhaps with even more sprays added to the top tier for a final, grand flourish.

Materials and Equipment

Spray of wild poppy with bud and 2 leaves (see page 38)

Foxglove stem and 2 leaves (see page 50)

Honeysuckle flower (see page 44)

Wild rose spray, 2 wild rose leaf sprays and a wild rose hip (see page 56)

2 poppy leaves, taped together

Half-width Nile green flower tape (Hamilworth)

8in (20cm) round sugarpasted cake

Method

Attach a length of half-width Nile green tape to the spray of wild poppy.

Tape in the foxglove stem on the right-hand side, followed by a foxglove leaf.

Tape in the honeysuckle flower to the left of the central poppy.

Tape in a spray consisting of the wild rose, one wild rose leaf spray and the rose hip, below the poppy and to the right side.

Tape in the other spray of wild rose leaves on the left, behind and in between the poppy and honeysuckle.

Complete the spray with two poppy leaves and the remaining foxglove leaf positioned below the poppy.

Gladioli Spray

For this eye-catching spray, stunning pink and purple gladiolus flowers have been arranged with looped leaves, flower buds and aquilegia seed heads. A bold design such as this can be used for many different occasions and is best displayed on top of a very simple cake.

Materials and Equipment

6 looped gladioli leaves (see page 62)

2 magenta gladiolus flowers and 1 bud (see page 62)

3 sprays of aquilegia seed heads with 3 x 5 individual seed heads (see page 122)

1 violet gladiolus flower and 1 bud (see page 62)

Half-width Nile green flower tape (Hamilworth)

8in (20cm) round sugarpasted cake

Method

Tape together one looped leaf, the magenta gladiolus bud, one seed head spray and one magenta gladiolus flower.

Add a second looped leaf and violet gladiolus flower below and to the left.

Add a seed head spray in the centre.

Tape in the second magenta flower to the right, followed by a seed head spray behind this flower and a looped leaf to the extreme right-hand side.

Tape in the violet-coloured bud underneath the magenta flower.

Complete the spray with three looped leaves taped evenly around the base of the spray.

Leave the stems loose.

Japanese Anemone Spray

This pretty semi-circular spray of pink and white Japanese anemones has delicate variegated ivy foliage to complement it. Four pink anemones have been dusted with dusky pink dusting powder and the edges of the petals with lavender dusting powder to produce the beautiful pale pink, shaded tones. It has been designed to sit on top of a 9in (22.5cm) round sugarpasted cake.

Materials and Equipment

6 small, 12 medium and 4 large varigated ivy leaves (see page 118)

9 medium Japanese anemone leaves (see page 70)

1 white Japanese anemone (see page 70)

4 pink Japanese anemones (see page 70)

Dusky pink and lavender dusting powders (EdAble Art)

Half-width beige and Nile green flower tapes

24# white Sunrise wires for assembly

9in (22.5cm) round sugarpasted cake

Method

Make six sprays of variegated ivy, using one small, two medium and one large ivy leaf taped together with half-width beige flower tape in each spray.

Make three sprays of three Japanese anemone leaves, comprising one large and two small leaves, using half-width Nile green flower tape.

Attach a length of 24# white wire to the base of one of the variegated ivy sprays.

For the left-hand spray, tape down the stem and add a Japanese anemone leaf spray to the left side; tape down the stem and add a pink flower to the centre and a ivy stem to the left side; tape down the stem adding another pink flower and another ivy stem to the right side.

Repeat this process for the right side, reversing the position of the flowers and leaves and adding the white flower and Japanese anemone leaf spray to the base.

Bend the stems of each spray to 90 degrees and tape them together.

Place the finished spray in an upright position on top of the cake.

Old-Fashioned Roses and Ivy

This gorgeous, elegant cake topper has been created to adorn a wedding or anniversary cake. The stylish David Austin-type roses have been very popular with brides for their bridal bouquets. Here they have been used alongside variegated ivy, looped leaves, laurustinus flowers, aquilegia seed heads dusted with aubergine, and finished with rose leaves and loops of pale pink wire.

Materials and Equipment

4 stems of variegated ivy, consisting of 1 small, 2 medium and 1 large leaf (see page 118)

3 stems of aquilegia seed heads dusted with aubergine dusting powder (EdAble Art) (see page 122)

2 looped leaves (see Gladiolus, page 62)

2 laurustinus flower heads (see page 104)

3 old-fashioned roses (see page 76)

3 stems rose leaves (see page 76)

2 heart-shaped pale pink wire loops

Half-width Nile green flower tape (Hamilworth)

Aubergine dusting powder (EdAble Art)

4 x lengths 26# pale pink wire (Hamilworth)

Fine-nosed pliers

Posy pick

6in (15cm) round sugarpasted cake

Method

Attach a length of half-width Nile green flower tape to a stem of variegated ivy, a seed head spray and two heart-shaped wire loops.

Tape in two looped leaves to surround this stem.

Tape in two laurustinus flower heads at this same point, then tape down the stem.

Tape in three roses, one at a time, evenly spaced around the stem.

Tape in a seed head spray in between the roses, followed by three ivy and rose leaf sprays.

Place the completed spray in a posy pick that has been inserted into the centre of the cake.

Pull the leaf stems down with a pair of fine-nosed pliers so that they sit over the edges of the cake.

Dahlia Spray

Uplifting lemon-yellow and vivid orange single dahlia flowers sit beautifully alongside bright-green leaves, making a fresh, sunny and joyful arrangement. This charming cake topper would be perfect for a Mother's Day celebration or the birthday of a keen gardener.

Materials and Equipment

1 orange dahlia and 1 bud (see page 84)

2 yellow dahlia and 2 buds (see page 84)

13 dahlia leaves (see page 89)

2 beige wire loops

Half-width Nile green flower tape (Hamilworth)

8in (20cm) round sugarpasted cake

Method

Make three sprays of leaves with one leaf at the top and two leaves immediately below and side by side.

Make one spray of leaves with two leaves and two sprays with one leaf.

Attach a length of half-width tape to the stem below a yellow flower. Tape in the orange bud and a three-leaf spray. Attach a yellow bud to the right-hand side and behind the flower. Tape down the stem.

Tape in the second yellow bud and a one-leaf spray and wire loop to the right-hand side.

Tape in a one-leaf spray in the centre, underneath the first yellow flower.

Tape in the orange flower and a three-leaf spray below the first flower and to the left.

Tape in the second yellow flower and a three-leaf spray to the right and at the same level as the orange flower.

Complete the spray with a beige looped wire in the centre and a two-leaf spray taped in below and to the left side. Leave the stems free.

Position the dahlia spray on top of a cake covered with sugarpaste.

Clematis Arrangement

These large, dramatic clematis flowers have been combined with sleek clematis buds and leaves, then taped together in an open arrangement that mimics their natural growing habit. This very simple, flat spray has been used to decorate an 8in (20cm) white sugarpasted cake.

Materials and Equipment

1 semi-open lavender clematis flower, 1 open flower and 3 buds (see page 90)

7 small and 9 medium-sized clematis leaves (see page 90)

24# white Sunrise wires (The Old Bakery)

Half-width Nile green flower tape (Hamilworth)

Fine-nosed pliers

8in (20cm) round sugarpasted cake

Method

Make sprays of leaves and buds and individual leaves as follows:

1. six small leaves and one bud;
2. one bud and one medium leaf;
3. two large separate leaves;
4. two sprays of two small and two medium leaves;
5. one small, two medium and one bud.

Attach a length of half-width Nile green tape to the base of spray 1, and tape down the stem for 1in (2.5cm).

Tape in the semi-open flower onto the stem, followed by spray 2 on the right-hand side.

Tape in the pair of large leaves (item 3) on either side of the stem at this point.

Tape down the stem for 1in (2.5cm), tape in the large open flower onto the stem, followed by two sprays (item 4) on either side of the stem.

Tape down the stem for ½in (1cm) then tape in the final leaf and bud spray (item 5).

Bend the stem to give a semi-circular spray, and place the spray on top of the cake

Hellebore Spray

Beautiful, complementary shades have been used in this stunning spray of hellebores, buds and foliage. Texture is provided by the laurustinus flowers and berry sprays and the aquilegia seed heads. It is finished with Italian arum leaves. This lovely medium-sized arrangement has been laid flat on top of a cake, but it could also be placed in a flower pick and inserted into the cake.

Materials and Equipment

3 Italian arum leaves (see page 110)

7 sprays of aquilegia seed heads (see page 122)

2 sprays of laurustinus flower heads and berry sprays (see page 104)

2 hellebores and 2 buds with leaves (see page 96)

Half-width Nile green flower tape (Hamilworth)

Small-nosed pliers

8in (20cm) round sugarpasted cake

Method

Attach a length of tape to two Italian arum leaves.

Position a spray of seed heads and a spray of laurustinus flowers behind these and tape them together to form a stem.

Tape in two hellebore flowers with buds and leaves onto the stem in the centre (one to the left side of the stem and one to the right-hand side).

Tape in two sprays of seed heads onto the stem to the left of the flowers and a spray of berries to the right.

Position two sprays of seed heads in the centre of the spray, then tape in another two sprays of seed heads to the right-hand side of the spray and just below the hellebore flower.

Tape in a spray of laurustinus berries and a spray of laurustinus flowers onto the stem below the flowers. Tape in an Italian arum leaf at the base of the stem to complete the spray.

Templates

Copy at 100%

Italian arum leaf

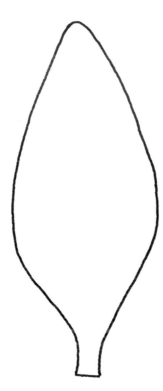

Foxglove leaf

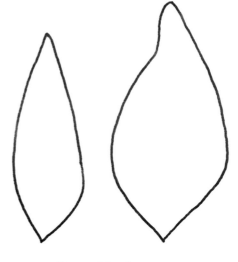

Ground ivy leaves

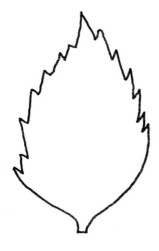

Dahlia leaf

Dahlia petal

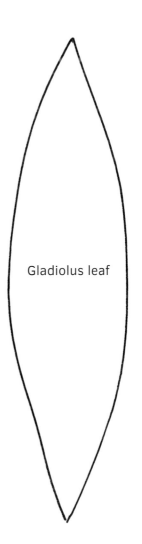

Gladiolus leaf

Hellebore leaves

Honeysuckle leaf

Gladiolus sheath

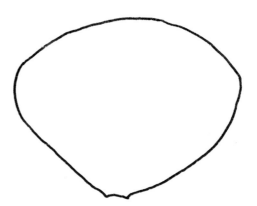

Red poppy petal

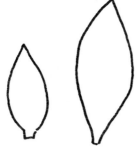

Laurustinus leaf

Wild rose petal

Suppliers

UK

A Piece of Cake
(Commercial flower paste and sugarcraft products, including Ellen Bosboom's veiners)
18–20 Upper High Street
Thame
Oxon
OX9 3EX
+44 (0)1844 213428
www.sugaricing.com

CelCakes
(Cel products, boards, pins and foam pad)
Walbut Mill Farm
Thornton
YO42 4RH
+44 (0)1759 318421
www.celcrafts.com

EdAble Art
(Dusting colours)
+44 (0)1388 816309
www.edableartworldofcolour.co.uk

Fine Cut Sugarcraft
(Cutters)
Workshop 4, Old Stable Block
Holme Pierrepont Hall
Holme Pierrepont
Nottingham
NG12 2LD
+44 (0)1159 334349
www.finecutsugarcraft.com

Squires Kitchen
(Veiners and dusting colours)
3 Waverley Lane
Farnham
Surrey
GU9 8BB
+44 (0)330 2234466
www.squires-shop.com

The Old Bakery
(Japanese Sunrise wires and stamens)
Kingston St Mary
Taunton
Somerset
TA2 8HW
+44 (0)1823 451205
www.oldbakery.co.uk

Tinkertech Two
(Cutters)
27 Florence Road
Parkstone
Poole
BH14 9JF
+44 (0)1202 738049
www.tinkertechtwo.com

US

Cake Crafts
(Dusting powders, cutters, veiners, wires and tapes)
4105 South Broadway
Englewood
CO 80113
+1 (303) 761 1522
www.cakecrafts.net

Cake Supplies USA
(Modelling tools)
715 Lakepointe Centre Dr.
Suite 101
O'Fallon, IL 62269
+1 618 477 2198
www.cakesuppliesusa.com

eCakeSupply
(Stamens, wires and tapes)
12225 SW 128th St Suite 106,
Miami FL 33186
+1 305 383 4238
www.ecakesupply.com

Global Sugar Art
(Tools, cutters and FMM sugarcraft products)
1509 Military Turnpike,
Plattsburgh
NY 12901
+1 518 561 3039
www.globalsugarart.com

About the Author

Marilyn Hill's interest in sugarcraft began more than 30 years ago when she attended her first class, and started making sugar flowers when cutters for flowers and leaves first became available. Marilyn joined the British Sugarcraft Guild in 1983 and is an honorary member, past president and past chairman. She is also a judge and an accredited demonstrator for the Guild. Passing on her skills to others is something Marilyn enjoys immensely through teaching flower-making classes, workshops and skill schools, and now this, her first book.

Acknowledgements

I would like to thank my husband Martin for his continued support and encouragement while I have been writing this book. I am indebted to Jonathan Bailey of GMC for his initial interest and helpful guidance in the contents of the book and to Dominique Page for her patience and sound advice. The beautiful photographs of my flowers and foliage have been produced by Ryan Braidley of Ryan Braidley Photography. His attention to detail and patience during the long photographic sessions was exemplary. I am so pleased and grateful for the lovely results he achieved with my work. Finally, I would like to acknowledge the British Sugarcraft Guild. Through this organization I have met and worked with many talented sugarcrafters who have offered encouragement and support in the pursuance of this project.

Index

First published 2019 by
Guild of Master Craftsman Publications Ltd, **Castle** Place, 166 High Street,
Lewes, **East** Sussex BN7 1XU

Text © Marilyn Hill, 2019

Copyright in the Work © GMC Publications Ltd, 2019

ISBN 978 1 78494 521 3

A catalogue record for this book is available from the British Library.

Publisher Jonathan Bailey
Production Jim Bulley and Jo Pallett
Senior Project Editor Dominique Page
Editor Nicola Hodgeson
Managing Art Editor Gilda Pacitti
Designer Luana Gobbo
Illustrator Marilyn Hill
Photographer Ryan Braidley
Colour origination by GMC Reprographics
Printed and bound in China

To order a book, or to request a catalogue, contact:
GMC Publications Ltd, Castle Place, 166 High Street,
Lewes, East Sussex BN7 1XU, United Kingdom
Tel: +44 (0)1273 488005
www.gmcbooks.com